D0006882

Ruminations on a Parrot Named Cosmo

By Betty Jean Craige

Author of *Conversations with Cosmo:*
At Home with an African Grey Parrot

SHERMAN ASHER PUBLISHING   Santa Fe

Copyright © 2021 Betty Jean Craige

No part of this book may be reproduced
without the permission of the publisher
except for brief passages used for reviews.

ISBN 978-1-890932-51-0

Library of Congress Control Number: 2020951162

Title page photo by Nancy Evelyn
Text and cover design by James Mafchir
Edited by Cinny Green

Sherman Asher Publishing
P.O. Box 31752
Santa Fe, NM 87594-1725
www.shmanasher.com westernedge@santa-fe.net

Printed in Canada

To my friends who love Cosmo

Acknowledgments

I thank The Athens Banner-Herald for carrying my column "Cosmo Talks" from December 2011 through November 2013 and for giving me permission to publish a book based on those essays.

I thank Susan Tate, Margaret Anderson, Hugh Ruppersburg, and many other friends, acquaintances, and strangers for their enthusiastic response to my stories of Cosmo.

I thank Nancy Evelyn, Chuck Murphy, and Alvaro Santistevan for their photographs of Cosmo and me.

I thank Cinny Green, my editor at Sherman Asher Publishing, for her profound knowledge of the English language, her skillful editing, and her love of Cosmo.

I thank Jim Mafchir, my publisher and friend, for helping me share Cosmo with others through two books: Conversations with Cosmo: At Home with an African Grey Parrot and Ruminations on a Parrot Named Cosmo.

And, I thank Cosmo, my talkative, funny, mischievous, clever, deceptive, affectionate, dearly beloved African Grey parrot, for giving me two decades of joy and hilarity.

Contents

PART II: **Cosmo and Her Fellow Residents of Earth**

PART I

Cosmo, An African Grey Parrot

Photo by Chuck Murphy

CHAPTER 1

Introduction

Cosmo: "Come here!"
Betty Jean: "Okay, Cosmo. I'm coming."
Cosmo: "Come here! Cosmo wanna go up!"
Betty Jean: "I'm coming Cosmo. Just a minute."
Cosmo: "Cosmo wanna poop."

COSMO BECKONS ME at dawn. That's how I wake up. She expects me to come into her room immediately. She wants me to let her out of her roost cage, carry her into my still dark bedroom, and set her on the rope perch atop the large cage there to do her morning poop. Then, bless her, she stays quiet while I go back to bed for a few more minutes of sleep.
After a half hour or so, she says, "How are you?" or "I love you." And she begins whistling.

Cosmo is a Congo African grey parrot. She talks meaningfully, she laughs appropriately, she expresses emotions like mine, and she makes jokes. And she whistles. African greys are considered among the smartest parrots, the most talkative, and the most capable of mimicking accurately the human voice. Cosmo is no exception.

Cosmo awakens happy to start the day and eager to learn what awaits her. She whistles a medley of her favorite tunes: "Heigh-Ho," "Bridge on the River Kwai," and "Meow Mix." She repeats the calls of the birds in our neighborhood.

During the day she tells me when it's time to do something like "Time to go to kitchen" or "Time for shower for Betty Jean."

She asks where I'm "gonna go." She asks whether she can go too: "Cosmo wanna go to work? Okay? Cosmo we're gonna go in a car?" Periodically she says, "I love you," "Cosmo wanna kiss," "Betty Jean wanna kiss feathers?" and "I wanna cuddle."

I can locate Cosmo by whistling the first few bars of one of her tunes and waiting for her to complete it. She usually does.

She loves to whistle duets with me, even at the expense of being discovered in her hiding place. She'll ask, "Cosmo and Betty Jean wanna whi-hul?" "Whistle" is one of the few words she can't pronounce correctly. She'll do the first line of "Yankee Doodle" or "Heigh-Ho" or "Bridge on the River Quai" and look at me expectantly. I'll do the second line, she'll do the third, and I'll finish up. Cosmo knows I will whistle my parts. That's the deal.

I bought Cosmo, then six months old, from a local pet store in May of 2002, for intellectual reasons. I had always wondered how individuals of other species saw the world, and I figured that a parrot could tell me.

When friends asked why I'd brought a parrot into my dog-centered household, I replied that a parrot seemed easier to care for than a dolphin or a gorilla.

In her first year of life, Cosmo did not talk. But she mimicked many household sounds: the microwave, the telephone, the smoke alarm, and the squeaks of cabinet doors as well as the bark of the dogs, the chatter of the squirrels, and the many different chirps and caws of the birds that fed off the deck railing outside her window.

I spoke to her constantly, in simplified English, of course, and gave her lots of cuddling. I'd say, "Cosmo is a good bird," "Cosmo wanna kiss?" "Cosmo wanna go to kitchen?" "Cosmo wanna shower?" "Cosmo wanna cuddle?" and "I love you."

I did not say "Betty Jean loves you" or "Betty Jean wanna shower" or "Betty Jean wanna kiss." She had to learn my name on her own.

One evening in December of 2002, Cosmo said softly from atop the cage in my bedroom, "Bird." I was astonished. She was quiet for a few minutes, and then she said, "Cosmo is a bird."

I leapt out of my chair, exclaiming, "Cosmo is a good bird!

I love you! I wanna kiss!" She leaned forward for me to kiss her warm black beak.

That was just the beginning. Within a year Cosmo had learned my name; had told her first joke—"Telephone for bird!"—which made both of us laugh uproariously; had begun using her vocabulary to make new phrases, such as "shower for Betty Jean room," by which she meant my bathroom; and had figured out the difference between a statement and a question.

By the age of six Cosmo had acquired a documented vocabulary of more than a hundred and sixty-five words, which she employed appropriately. My Christmas card of 2008 reported the following utterances that are part of my daily conversations with Cosmo:

Betty Jean go in a car Betty Jean has clothes Come here, Mary Cosmo don't wanna go to kitchen Cosmo wanna be a good bird Cosmo wanna cuddle Cosmo wanna go in a car, okay? Cosmo wanna go to Betty Jean room Cosmo wanna go to Cosmo room Cosmo wanna go up— okay? Cosmo wanna good kiss Cosmo wanna peanut Cosmo wanna poop Doggies wanna go for a walk Doggies wanna go in a car Doggies, come here! Good shower! Wow! I love you! I wanna kiss I wanna shower and a peanut Look, squirrel! Mary is a doggie Move! Ow! Peanut Play ball Please! Shower for Betty Jean room Stay here! Telephone for Betty Jean! Telephone for bird! Hehehehehe Thank you That hurt! That hurt? That's bark That's bad doggie! That's shower for Betty Jean That's television There you are! Time for shower and a peanut for Cosmo! Time for shower for Betty Jean! Time to go to bed for Cosmo Wanna be a good bird Wanna cuddle? Wanna dance? Wanna go back in cage Wanna go to bed? Wanna go to kitchen? We're gonna go in a car We're gonna go to Betty Jean bedroom We're gonna go to Cosmo room We're gonna go to kitchen We're gonna have company! What a bird! What's Cosmo? Cosmo is a birdie What?

What's that? What's that? That's Cosmo Where are you?
Where gonna go? Where wanna gonna go? Where's
Cosmo? Woo woo woo! That's doggie bark Wow! Good
shower! Wow! Good kiss! Yes Yoohoo! You have
reached 549-6243 You have reached Betty Jean! You have
reached Cosmo! Hehehehehe You wanna kiss? You
wanna dance? Back in cage Ball Be back soon Betty
Jean go in a car Betty Jean has clothes Betty Jean wanna
kiss a beak? Betty Jean wanna kiss feathers? Betty Jean
wanna whistle? Bird Birdie Birdie has feathers Bye
Come Come here Come here please Come here, Mary
Come on Come up here Come, Mary! Cosmo Cosmo
and Betty Jean wanna talk? Cosmo and Betty Jean wanna
whistle? Cosmo bad bird? Cosmo go back in cage?
Cosmo be a good bird—okay? Cosmo don't bite—okay?
Cosmo don't wanna go to kitchen Cosmo go back in cage

Now this adorable sixteen-ounce, six-inch-tall, grey-and-red-feathered funny parrot and I love each other.

And when she teases me the way I tease her or laughs the way I laugh, at the very same things I find funny, I say she's a lot like me.

Oh, my.

Has Cosmo taken on my personality from living with me, or have I taken on hers? Does she think like me, or do I think like her? We certainly sound alike. My friends accuse me of saying "Hello" with Cosmo's intonation of joyous enthusiasm. Guilty.

Here is the question I ponder: Has our proximity to our household pets made us more like each other mentally? Do birds—and gorillas, dolphins, squirrels, and deer—actually have thoughts, feelings, desires, fears, and expectations similar to our own, whether or not they live with us?

In that case, we have extraordinarily underestimated the intelligence and emotions of all the feathery, furry, and hairy animals who populate our planet. On the assumption that we humans are the only smart ones around, we have probably mistreated them.

Contemplate this: Humans are a small fraction of the trillions of animals on Earth whose lives are shaped by thoughts and feelings and memories. Thoughts about what to do, whom to chase, whom to mate, where to find food, where to shelter. Feelings of fear, affection, joy. Memories of their fellow creatures, of their close calls. And memories of what we humans have done to them. Everybody's thinking. If they all thought aloud, we'd have a mighty noisy planet.

Cosmo doesn't know the life-or-death physical excitement that her wild cousins in the rain forest of the Congo experience daily. She has never seen a hawk snatch an African grey from a tree branch. She's never seen a monkey steal eggs out of a nest. She's never seen a flock of African greys take flight.

And she's never foraged for food, or mated, or laid an egg, or raised a chick. She is from Florida, from a commercial aviary.

Cosmo hatched in December of 2001 after a twenty-eight-day incubation period. I don't know the exact date and time of her emergence from her egg, so I celebrate her hatchday on the winter solstice, the longest night of the year.

Of course the winter solstice is meaningless for Cosmo's relatives in the rain forests of the Congo Basin near the equator, because days and nights are approximately twelve hours long there throughout the year. Instead of winter and summer, the region has dry season and wet season. African greys tend to have conjugal bliss during dry season.

By the way, their act of mating is called a "cloacal kiss," whereby the male and the female press their cloacae together to allow the male to inject his sperm into the female. According to close, obviously very close, observers, both male and female appear to find mating pleasurable.

Like other species of parrots in the wild, African greys court their mates, marry for life, and form families. The hen lays two-to-four eggs in her tree hole nest, incubates them alone, and eats when her dutiful husband brings her dinner.

When the chicks hatch, the parents give each of them a signature call.

Then the parents keep their family together for a year while they educate them. They teach their chicks to speak, to be good citizens of the flock, to obey the laws of the jungle, and to thrive in the wild.

Imagine how distressed parrots must become when parrot poachers seize one of their family. The poachers do more than simply reduce the population of an endangered species when they capture birds for the pet trade. They bring anguish to the bird's parents, siblings, and offspring, who recognize their family members as individuals and miss them when they've been taken away.

Cosmo was not wildcaught, nor was she educated by her parrot parents. Her breeder, like parrot breeders everywhere, took her away from her parents when she was younger than five months old so that she'd be educated by human caregivers in the ways of a human household. She learned to talk because she was still in her learning period when she came to live with me.

Cosmo knows she's a bird. She recognizes herself in the mirror. And she recognizes "birdies" on the computer, which she calls "television." So we watch the Berry College Eagles live web cam.

This morning Cosmo observed a crow fly into the eagles' vacated nest and begin foraging. The eagles must have left some tasty organic debris—mouse bones, squirrel tails and the like—when their two fledglings departed. The crow kept up a loud, continuous "caw, caw," and Cosmo answered equally loudly, "Caw, caw, caw."

I don't know whether Cosmo was speaking to the crow or cheering on the crow the way I cheer on the Georgia Bulldogs when I watch them on television.

Cosmo has taught me that she and I have much in common, and that we humans are not alone in having thoughts and feeling, that we humans have been mistaken in our assumption that we are intrinsically superior to other animals, and that the propensity to rank the intelligence of non-human animals on the basis of proximity to human intelligence is arrogant, self-centered, unwarranted, misguided, useless, dangerous, destructive, and downright ridiculous.

This is the theme of *Ruminations on a Parrot Named Cosmo* which originated in a Sunday column I wrote for *The Athens Banner-Herald* from 2011 to 2013 titled "Cosmo Talks." I had already published a book about Cosmo's learning to speak, *Conversations with Cosmo: At Home with an African Grey Parrot,* and I wanted to share anecdotes about Cosmo's hilarious antics with my local community. However, "Cosmo Talks" quickly evolved from accounts of Cosmo's activities to reflections on parrots' anatomy; birds' evolution from dinosaurs; the concept of nature; the evidence of consciousness in birds and mammals; the interdependence of all Earth's living organisms; and the similarities in mental life between humans and non-human animals.

When I wrote "Cosmo Talks" I had two dogs, Kaylee and Mary, with whom Cosmo played. Now I have Cosmo alone, and she plays with me. She just walked into my study.

"I are here," she announced.

CHAPTER 2

Names

COSMO HAD TALKED for eight months or so before she learned my name. She certainly knew hers so well that when a DNA test showed she was a female, I could not change it. She was already referring to herself in third person: "Cosmo wanna shower." "Cosmo wanna peanut." "Cosmo gonna poop."

Cosmo called my four dogs by name: Holly, Daisy, Blanche, whom she called "Blash," and Kaylee. This was a significant achievement since American Eskimo Dogs look a lot alike, at least to humans. A few years later, my dogs numbered two: Kaylee and little Mary. Cosmo called Mary by name, and she changed Kaylee's name to "Kary," rhyming it with Mary.

If Mary went outside and barked, Cosmo would yell, "Mary, come here!"

Or she'd tattle on her, telling me, "Mary has bark."

Whenever I brought something new into the house, Cosmo would ask, "What's that?" I would reply, "broom," or "box," or "dinner for doggies." On the occasion that I brought in something familiar, she would say, "That's clothes," or "That's paper."

Cosmo knew that everything had a name, in human language.

But she did not know my name. I had not thought of referring to myself in third person. I should have.

So the morning I first told her it was "Time for shower for Betty Jean," after she had declared "Time for shower for Cosmo," Cosmo appeared startled. She looked up at me from the floor—she is five feet shorter than I am—and repeated, "B'Jean! Time for shower for B'Jean!" Now she knew my name!

Soon thereafter she would shout, "Telephone for B'Jean,"

when the phone rang, and "B'Jean, come here," when she was in another room. Once I began enunciating my name clearly, "Betty Jean," she corrected her pronunciation.

According to Cornell University scientist Karl Berg, who studied green-rumped parrots in Venezuela, parrot parents give each chick in the clutch a different signature call. That is, they name them. The chicks learn their names and use their names to refer to themselves. They use each other's name to refer to each other in the flock.

Biologists at the University of St. Andrews in Scotland have discovered that dolphins and whales use signature calls. Bottlenose dolphins develop their own signature whistles and recognize those of their fellow pod members. Sperm whales announce themselves to each other by a personal identifier, a unique set of clicks, at the beginning of their vocalization.

Is this really different from Cosmo's beginning her sentences with "Cosmo," as in "Cosmo wanna cuddle"?

Apparently, naming is not an exclusively human activity.

Nor is vocal communication, obviously.

My friends Wyatt and Margaret regularly invite Cosmo to dinner. Cosmo speaks to them differently from the way she speaks to me. When Cosmo hears Wyatt's voice, she greets him with the warble that he uses to greet her. Maybe she considers the warble to be his signature call, or his name. When Cosmo hears Margaret's voice, she greets her with the trill that Margaret uses when she addresses Cosmo, "Cosmo-o-o-o-o!"

When men speak to her, Cosmo uses a low voice, a man's voice, to say, "How are you?" When she speaks on the telephone, Cosmo uses a guttural voice to say, "Hello." That must be the way phone speech sounds to her.

Cosmo knows that all the animals in her world, including humans, speak differently from each other. She does her best to communicate with all of us.

One day, while engrossed in my writing at the computer, I heard a loud rat-a-tat-tat. Without thinking, I asked Cosmo: "What's that?"

Cosmo replied: "That's birdie."

It was a pileated woodpecker. I named the woodpecker Watatatat.

Another day, Cosmo saw two black crows take off silently, and without hesitation she called out to them: "Caw caw!" She must have been pleased to hear them reply.

Cosmo knows that the large black crows, the medium-sized red and black woodpeckers, the smaller red cardinals, and the tiny yellow finches are all birds, like her sixteen-ounce, grey-and-red-feathered self.

The birds, dogs, cats, squirrels, bears, turtles, horses, and whales living with us on Earth all think about each other, recognize each other's calls, and even distinguish individuals from each other within a species. They have relationships we humans cannot fathom. Some of them have names.

Chapter 3

Internal Motivation

WHEN COSMO AND I visit elementary schools, the children will often request of me to "Make Cosmo talk" or "Make Cosmo get out of her cage."

I tell them, "I can't make Cosmo do anything."

Cosmo speaks meaningfully. But she doesn't speak on command. Actually, she doesn't do anything on command— not speak, not get out of her cage, not go to bed, not come out of the cabinet, not even be a good bird. She does what she likes, most of the time.

I've been asked, "How did you teach Cosmo to speak?" I have to reply, "I didn't teach her to speak. She learned on her own." Then I explain.

Cosmo learned to speak by listening to me speak to her. I used a simplified English in the months before she uttered her first word. I'd say, "Cosmo wanna peanut?" I'd give her a peanut. "Cosmo wanna go to kitchen?" I'd take her to the kitchen. "Cosmo wanna kiss?" I'd lift her up for a kiss. "Cosmo wanna cuddle?" We'd cuddle, and I'd say, "I love you" and "Cosmo is a good bird."

Whenever Cosmo said something to me, I said something back to her, but not the same thing. I gave her my full attention. I treated her like an important feathery little person. We conversed. That's how she expanded her vocabulary.

I never asked Cosmo to repeat a word after me. I never gave her a treat for performing. She is not a performer.

Cosmo spoke because she wanted to speak. Her only incentive to speak was the desire to communicate with me. Her only reward for speaking was the pleasure of communicating with me.

She loved me. She still does. I love her. I think that all Earth's residents want to communicate with those they love.

Recently, retired University of Georgia elementary education professor Penny Oldfather told me that I was exemplifying an educational principle dear to her heart: individuals develop intellectually and creatively more when they are motivated by their own interests and curiosity than when they are motivated by external rewards.

In fact, Penny said much current research shows that "extrinsic rewards reduce intrinsic motivations, because extrinsic rewards focus the learner's attention on the reward."

This research challenges the performance-oriented educational philosophy that children need rewards for learning.

I agree with Penny. I'd put it this way: To give Cosmo peanuts for saying the right word after me would reward mimicry and reduce conversation. Cosmo might learn to say "Go, Dawgs!" but not "Where Betty Jean wanna gonna go?"

Cosmo was motivated to speak not solely because I was her significant other who spoke to her. Cosmo was adapting to a cultural environment in which speech gave her some control over her life. She could ask for peanuts and kisses and obtain them. She could tell me what she wanted to do, and she knew I'd usually say, "Okay." She could bark with the dogs and call the dogs to her. She could get people to laugh. She could make her own life interesting, even when she was "back in cage."

Speech was the means to participate in my culture. Cosmo wanted to participate. Of course.

I have learned much from my dear, funny, mischievous, self-confident, self-motivated, obviously happy bird. But maybe the greatest lesson she's taught me through her love of learning is that, most likely, every other feathery, furry, or hairy, or even scaly resident of Earth has curiosity too.

Last night as I was preparing to go out, Cosmo and I had this extended conversation:

Cosmo: "Where Betty Jean wanna gonna go?"

Betty Jean: "Betty Jean gonna go to dinner."

Cosmo: "Betty Jean and Cosmo gonna go in a car?"

Betty Jean: "No. Betty Jean gonna go in a car. Cosmo gonna stay home with doggies."

Cosmo: "Doggies gonna go for a walk?"

Betty Jean: "No, doggies gonna stay home with Cosmo."

Cosmo: (muttering to herself) "Betty Jean gonna go to work."

Cosmo: (out loud) "Good-bye."

Betty Jean: "Good-bye, Cosmo. Good-bye, doggies. I love you."

Chapter 4

A Sense of Humor

Cosmo: "Doggies gonna go for a walk?"
Betty Jean: "Yes. Doggies gonna go for a walk with Betty Jean."
Cosmo: "Cosmo gonna go for a walk! Hahahaha! Nooooo. Cosmo is a bird."

COSMO IS AN INTELLECTUAL, at least by avian standards, for she enjoys mental activity as much as physical activity. She gets fun simply from talking to me.

Although she likes to chase the dogs, pull out lipsticks and eyeliners from my cosmetic drawer, pull out pots and pans from the kitchen cabinets, pull out books from my bookshelves, destroy my phonebooks, remove the tops of pens and highlighters, and walk on the dining room table to eat off guests' plates, all to amuse herself, she prefers to perch atop a cage and amuse me.

Cosmo teases me, tells her jokes, and laughs at her jokes— all to amuse me. She loves to make me laugh, and to laugh with me. She gets pleasure out of giving me pleasure. How fortunate can I be!

When I kiss Mary, my little American Eskimodog, Cosmo will say, "Mary has feathers," and laugh loudly. I laugh loudly too. Then she'll say, "Noooo. Mary has fur."

She'll bark, "Woo woo woo," perfectly mimicking the dogs' bark, and then say, "That's Cosmo! Hehehe."

I chuckle, "Hehehe."

She'll call me, "Betty Jean wanna kiss feathers? Come here!" I say "Okay," and go to her. She'll climb out of reach and say, "Nooooo. Hahahaha!"

Cosmo laughs and chuckles just the way I do. She got her laugh and her chuckle from me.

However, what is more interesting is that Cosmo, like many parrots, laughs at appropriate times and without my prompting.

From the day she joined my family, Cosmo has observed the effect of words on her environment. I call the dogs to get them to come to me. So she calls them, "Yoohoo, doggies come here," to get them to come to her. The dogs once did, but now they don't.

I shout, "Doggies wanna go for a walk?" and the dogs run to me, so Cosmo shouts, "Doggies wanna go for a walk?" to get them to run to her. The dogs once did, but now they don't.

Since I routinely say, "Telephone for Betty Jean," and hurry to the phone when I hear the phone's ring, Cosmo mimics the phone's ring to get me to hurry to the room where she is. I once did, but now I don't. However, I do laugh at her efforts, and so does she.

Cosmo knows well that words—in English, a foreign language to her—have consequences.

Humor requires an awareness of the difference between what is normal and what is strange or out of place. Cosmo's utterances ""Telephone for Cosmo" and "Cosmo gonna go for a walk" show her awareness that the normal situation is "Telephone for Betty Jean" and "Doggies gonna go for a walk."

For Cosmo, just as for a young human, it's a short step from realizing what utterances are normal to realizing what utterances are strange or out of place, and therefore humorous.

It's another step entirely to initiate humor, to create situations that make individuals laugh. Cosmo has to know not only the difference between what is normal and what is out of place, but also the difference between what is harmlessly out of place that I will find funny and what is out of place that I will not like.

When she overturns the wastebasket, spilling its contents on the floor, Cosmo does not laugh. Instead, she immediately looks up at me to see what I will do about the situation. Or she hurries away from the scene of her crime. She can distinguish being funny from being bad.

Skeptics may argue that Cosmo has simply learned from me what utterances elicit laughter. But I believe that Cosmo herself finds situations funny, that she has a sense of humor.

If that is the case, do other non-human animals like dogs, squirrels, dolphins, gorillas, and crows also have a sense of humor?

Cosmo's sense of humor is verbal because she inhabits a world of words, my world. Being able to talk, she can have fun just talking, like us humans.

As I write, Cosmo is perched on her cage behind me discussing her body: "Cosmo has a beak. Cosmo has feathers. Cosmo has feet."

Uh oh. Now she is climbing down from the cage and heading toward my bedroom. I beg her, "Cosmo, please be a good bird!"

Cosmo answers, "Noooo! Cosmo don't wanna be a good bird. Hehehehe!"

CHAPTER 5

House Rules

SOME YEARS AGO, my sixteen-ounce African rey parrot Cosmo noticed my thirty-pound American Eskimo dog Blanche following her closely down the hall. When Blanche sniffed her tail feathers, Cosmo turned her head around and reprimanded her, "No, no, no, no!" And then continued waddling toward the kitchen.

Startled by the reprimand from a bird, Blanche skedaddled. She looked embarrassed.

Cosmo knows the house rules. I make most of them, but she makes a few. No sniffing tail feathers is her rule.

Other rules are No barking, biting, or jumping by dogs. One weekend I puppy-sat my nephew's hyperactive three-month-old English Setter Sally. From her perch on her dining room cage, Cosmo observed Sally jump up and down, spin in circles, and nip my hand in her wild excitement over being fed. Cosmo exclaimed, "No, No, No! Bad doggie!"

These days, when I take a nap on the sofa in her room, Cosmo watches over me quietly from atop her roost cage. She has learned that if she is a good, good bird, does not talk while I'm dozing, and does not climb down, she can stay on top of her cage for my forty-five-minute nap. That's one rule I made that Cosmo tends to obey.

If the dogs jump on me and wake me up, she scolds them: "Doggies, no, no, no! Doggies, move!" If they go outside and bark, she calls them: "Doggies, come here!" Cosmo assumes that she is the enforcer when I'm asleep.

Cosmo did not take long to learn what is permitted and what is prohibited in my household. She knows clearly when she is breaking the rules. She has a sense of right and wrong.

Of course, knowing the rules leads to deceiving the enforcer of the rules. I'm the enforcer when I'm awake. When I catch Cosmo doing something particularly bad, I say, "No, no, no!" and put her back in her cage.

Another of my rules is no destroying the baseboards.

One Sunday morning, I saw Cosmo enter the laundry room, where she customarily takes a big, splashy bird bath in the dogs' large water bowl. On most occasions she'll beckon me to view her fun. "Betty Jean, Come here! Cosmo wanna shower!" And after a dip, she'll say, "Wow, good shower! Cosmo wanna kiss!"

You can see her on the YouTube channel: https://www.youtube.com/user/cosmotalks.

But that morning, Cosmo was very quiet. I heard her working away at the baseboards, and I knew I'd find a pile of sawdust there. I hollered, "Cosmo, what are you doing?"

She hollered back, "Cosmo wanna shower. Look! Come here!"

As I walked down the hallway, I heard the quick pitter-patter of her toenails on the linoleum floor. Tic tac tic tac. By the time I got to the laundry room, she was climbing onto the water dish.

"Look!" she exclaimed. "Cosmo wanna shower! Good bird!"

Sure enough, there was sawdust all over the floor and not a drop of water. But I went along with her deception. "Cosmo wanna shower? Good bird," I said.

"I love you," she said. "Betty Jean wanna kiss? Smooooch."

"Smooch." I returned to my desk.

Then I heard her scurry back to the baseboard, chuckling, "Hehehehe."

I didn't scold her. I myself was chuckling at the pride Cosmo took in outsmarting me.

What had to go through Cosmo's mind for her to deceive me? Cosmo had to know what I expected of her. In this case it was to take a bird bath and not to chew the baseboards. She had to know that I would put her back into her cage if I caught her breaking the No-destroying-the-baseboards rule. She had to know that would please me watching her take her "shower" and also what would annoy me.

And she had to think she was smarter than I and that therefore she could fool me. And she knew I'd be happy if she told me she loved me.

She had empathy.

The *Cambridge Dictionary* defines empathy as "the ability to share someone else's feelings or experiences by imagining what it would be like to be in that person's situation."

Although I am not a linguist or a psychologist or an animal behaviorist, I'm convinced that language is the basis of empathy. It enables individuals to learn not only about themselves but also about each other.

Therefore, is empathy, which is the basis for love as we humans know it, also the basis for lying? And manipulation?

When I gave Cosmo my language, that is, a simplified version of English, I gave her my way of thinking about the world. I gave her access to my thoughts and the ability to communicate her own thoughts. I gave her my voice and, apparently, my sense of humor. I gave her my ideas of right and wrong, although apparently I didn't give her a strong conscience. And I gave her the ability to tell me something untrue.

In short, I gave her the ability to anticipate my behavior.

So if Cosmo knows the difference between right and wrong, does she have a sense of morality? The Random House Dictionary defines morality as "conformity to the rules of right conduct." If Cosmo knows the rules and doesn't always conform to them, as when she is a "bad bird," does she have a touch of immorality in her?

Marc Bekoff defines morality in his book *Wild Justice* as "a suite of interrelated other-regarding behaviors that cultivate and regulate social interactions." In other words, morality enables social animals including humans and wolves and all the other non-human animals who live together in packs, flocks, herds, gaggles to get along with each other. It is an aspect of cooperation.

Cosmo may have a sense of morality but she has no feelings of guilt. If she bites me, breaking the no-biting rule, she says cheerfully, without a hint of remorse, "That hurt? Cosmo bad bird go back in cage."

CHAPTER 6

Affection

I HAD HAD LIVED WITH COSMO for only two months when I took her back to the pet store to get her flight feathers clipped. As soon as she exited her car cage, Cosmo spotted the other baby African grey parrot who had been her companion before I bought her and separated them. Cosmo leaned forward, almost falling off my hand in her eagerness to join her clutch mate. The other chick was just as eager, and the two birds rushed to each other on the perch and put their little black tongue into each other's open beak. They kissed.

The birds' obvious recognition of each other and their mutual affection meant that they must have missed each other when I broke them up. I felt sad. I had never considered Cosmo's emotional attachments when I purchased her. In fact, I had not given a single thought to the possibility that these young birds had thoughts and feelings.

Since then Cosmo has made her emotional life quite evident in my household, where she is very attentive to my dogs Mary and Kaylee. A few years ago, Mary had to spend a week at the vet's office. The second day that I came home without Mary, Cosmo asked, "Mary go in a car?" That was probably the only way she could ask why Mary was not home. I told her, "Yes, Mary go in a car. Mary come home soon." Cosmo missed Mary. She had been thinking about her.

On Friday evening, I brought Mary home. Cosmo immediately climbed down from her cage and followed the sick little dog under the bed to greet her. "Hi!" she said excitedly, fully confident that Mary had missed her too.

When I play Il Divo's gorgeous rendition of "Nights in White Satin"—loudly, because I love it—Cosmo starts whistling like crazy. Sometimes she will say, "Cosmo wanna dance!" I take her on my left wrist and swing her back and forth to the rhythm of the song. After a minute or two she will say either "Cosmo wanna cuddle" or "Cosmo wanna kiss."

Betty Jean wanna do both.

Scientists have only recently begun studying emotions in non-human animals. In our centuries-long tradition of considering humans unique in our intelligence and our capacity for love and sorrow, we have ignored the signs that non-human animals had feelings like ours. But now we're seeing evidence that lots of Earth's creatures, human and non-human alike, have emotional lives. We know that dogs, cats, parrots, elephants, chimpanzees, and tigers are capable of affection and, if so, then they must also have a capacity for grief, like humans.

Cosmo shows affection when she asks for a kiss and puts her little beak up to my lips. She makes a tiny, barely audible smooch a millisecond before we touch. And she asks for a kiss at appropriate times. You may think that she learned to kiss from me, but when she kissed the other African grey at the pet store, she seemed to do it instinctively.

She did it on her first date with a younger grey named Ruby. When she saw Ruby, Cosmo said, "Hello," with great delight, and hurried over to Ruby to kiss her. Ruby reciprocated.

Do all animals show affection by kissing? On the web you can find pictures of giraffes, prairie dogs, squirrels, chipmunks, rabbits, pigs, lions, leopards, orangutans, horses, dolphins, doves, owls, and fish all kissing their mates. You can find pictures of a dog kissing a koi, a cat kissing a dog, a rabbit kissing a chick, and a lion kissing the woman who saved him from malnutrition six years ago whom he apparently loves. And humans kissing everybody under the sun. Kissing must be a universal sign of affection.

So is cuddling, of course.

When Cosmo and I cuddle, I hold her on my left hand close to my chest and stroke her back, very gently. Sometimes

I stroke her head and rub her neck and pull her tail feathers, very gently. She holds still and closes her eyes in pleasure. We do this for fifteen minutes or so at bedtime, her bedtime. Finally, she says, "Cosmo wanna go to bed."

One evening after cuddling, Cosmo started jerking her head back and forth. Then she leaned forward to kiss me and deposited in my mouth a peanut that she'd kept in her craw since dinner! Cosmo felt such love for me at that moment that she gave me the peanut she'd saved for herself. I felt touched by her gesture. I didn't swallow the peanut, but I could have. It was still in pretty good condition

CHAPTER 7

Fluency

COSMO MAKES GRAMMATICAL ERRORS. Sometimes, as English teachers would say, she butchers the English language. But at least it's English that she speaks, so we communicate with no problem.

One afternoon while watching me cook, Cosmo asked, "Company we're gonna have?"

People unfamiliar with these marvelous birds tend to consider parrots' speech simple mimicry. But Cosmo's speech is obviously meaningful. Her grammatical mistakes prove it. I had never said, "Company we're gonna have." So she must know what the word "company" and the phrase "we're gonna have" mean, regardless of their word order.

I do say "gonna." My apologies.

Not all African greys speak as well as Cosmo. Perhaps Cosmo is an exceptionally smart individual. Or perhaps she knows that I am always listening to her, responding to her, and expecting her to speak to me in English.

Cosmo invents new words on the basis of words she already knows. Here is a conversation we had one morning.

> Cosmo: "Cosmo is a good bird. Cosmo is a birdie."
> Betty Jean: "Yes, Cosmo is a good birdie.
> Cosmo: "Mary is a doggie."
> Betty Jean: "Look! Squirrel."
> Cosmo: "That's squirrelie."

In all my born days I had never used the word "squirrely."

When she began talking at the age of twelve months, Cosmo heard me refer to my dogs as both "dogs" and "doggies." She called herself a "bird" for a good while before she suddenly started saying "Cosmo is a birdie." I had never called her a birdie. Nor had any guest in my house, to my knowledge.

So when she invented the word "squirrelie," Cosmo was generalizing from her knowledge that "dog" and "doggie" were the same and that "bird" and "birdie" were the same. That's pretty impressive intellectual work for a bird! If I had done as well at two years of age, I would have been very proud of myself.

The day I took her back to the pet store to get her flight feathers clipped, Cosmo heard the dozens of chirping parakeets for sale and said to me, "That's birdies!" She must have figured out the plural of "birdy" from the word "doggies."

I realized that Cosmo understood her need to communicate with me in my language when she translated the sound that she was making into English to help me out. She had been saying, "Whooooosh whoooooosh." Puzzled, I asked her, "What's that?" "That's water," she answered. Sure enough: she was mimicking the sound of the water coming out of the faucet near her roost cage.

Whenever I fill her water bowl, I say to her, "That's water for cage."

She often says, "Cosmo wanna water for cage."

Cosmo not only uses my language, English, to talk with me, but she uses my language to talk to herself. She says, "Cosmo poop," when that's what she's just done. She murmurs, "That's doggie bark," when Mary is barking at passersby. She climbs onto the dogs' big water dish muttering, "Cosmo wanna shower," when I'm in the other part of the house.

Cosmo knows that "shower" has several meanings: the minimal mist bath I give her with a spray bottle; the big shower I give myself in the bathroom; and the bird bath she gives herself in the laundry room. So she must have deduced that "shower" means getting water all over one's body, no matter whose body it might be.

She knows that "paper" has more than one meaning as

well: "paper for cage," meaning the newspaper; "paper for Cosmo poop," also meaning a newspaper; "and "paper for Cosmo poop," meaning a paper towel. In my household we use lots of paper.

I know that English has become Cosmo's primary language because she amuses herself in English. I'm hearing her pretend to have a conversation on the telephone. In a voice barely distinguishable from mine, she has just said softly: "Hi, Joan. How are you? Fine, thank you. Wanna go for a walk? Okay. Good-bye. Beep." Joan is my dog-walking neighbor. After the beep Cosmo calls out to me, "That's Cosmo!" and laughs.

Language students know that they are not really fluent in a foreign language until they actually think in the foreign language, when they stop consciously translating. I would say that Cosmo is fluent in English

Photo by Betty Jean Craige

CHAPTER 8

Mirror

COSMO LOOKS AT HERSELF in the mirror and says, "That's Cosmo! Whatta bird!"

Mirror self-recognition in non-human animals is a big deal for scientists. Cosmo has recognized herself in the mirror for years, but only recently did I prove it, at least to the satisfaction of most people, though maybe not skeptical scientists. I created a YouTube video of Cosmo admiring herself in the mirror. To see her seeing herself go to: https//www.youtube.com/user/cosmotalks.

In an article on elephant self-recognition, a writer for *National Geographic News* (October 28, 2010) reported that researchers had placed a white X on an elephant's forehead that the elephant, Happy, could see only in a mirror. Happy touched the mark repeatedly with her trunk. She acted as if she knew that the X did not belong on her. Ergo, she must have known what she looked like without the X. This is the "mark test," which Happy passed.

The *National Geographic* reporter stated "Humans, great apes, and dolphins are the only other animals known to possess this form of self-awareness."

I would add parrots to the list.

I have other evidence that Cosmo knows what she looks like.

One Sunday, I was working at my computer. Cosmo was perched on top of her cage behind me, quietly preening. After an hour, I got tired of writing and pulled onto the computer screen an image of an American Eskimo dog—not one of mine, but one that looked like mine.

Cosmo suddenly said, "That's doggie!" She must have been keeping an eye on the screen.

I decided to test her by showing a photograph of her, of which I have hundreds, but by the time I had chosen one to put on the screen, Cosmo had climbed down from her cage and was heading down the hall to visit the dogs in my bedroom.

Cosmo is quite attentive to the computer, which she calls "television." So the next time she was on the cage behind me, I put up a video of her at the dogs' water bowl talking about taking a "shower." Cosmo looked sharply at the screen, first with one eye and then with the other, and declared, "That's a birdie! That's Cosmo!"

Cosmo had heard herself on audio CDs before. I have done a number of them to show company that Cosmo talks remarkably well. When Cosmo hears herself say something on the CD, she responds.

> Cosmo on CD: "Rrring rrring rrring. Telephone for Betty Jean!"
> Cosmo in real life: "Hello. How are you?" Cosmo on CD: "'We're gonna have company!"
> Cosmo in real life: "That's Cosmo! Cosmo is a bird."

Cosmo knows what she sounds like.

In one of her YouTube videos, Cosmo is perched on the towel rack above the sink in the bathroom. She looks at herself in the mirror. She says "Wanna kiss," leans forward, and pecks the mirror.

I set her on that rack to keep her out of trouble while I'm brushing my teeth, putting on make-up, and getting ready for the day.

When Cosmo looks at herself in the mirror, she'll say, "Cosmo is a birdie! Cosmo has feathers." Sometimes "Cosmo has a beak." Sometimes "Look, that's Cosmo. Cosmo is a good good bird!"

Occasionally, she'll raise a foot and ask, "What's that?" The answer, which she gives if I don't, is "That's feet."

She knows that "Cosmo has feathers. Mary has fur. Betty Jean has clothes."

This morning, as I write, Cosmo is talking to me non-stop, from inside her roost cage. I had to lock her up because she was getting into too much mischief for me to concentrate on this column. I won't go into details, but the mischief involved a telephone cord and a beak.

She calls me, "Where are you?"

I respond semi-consciously, "I'm here at Betty Jean's desk."

She sends me a very long kiss, "Smooooooch," and declares, "Wow, good kiss!" Then, she asks, "Betty Jean wanna dance?" I don't. "Betty Jean wanna kiss feathers?" I don't.

"I'm busy," I tell her.

So she mimics the ringing of the phone: "Rrring rrring rrring." I go into her room and pick up the receiver.

Cosmo laughs. "That's Cosmo," she says. "Whatta bird!"

Chapter 9

Annual Evaluation

COSMO JUST LEFT my study and waddled down the hall toward the kitchen, where the dogs were eating their dinner. As she entered the kitchen, Cosmo exclaimed to the dogs, "There you are!"

Cosmo says the same thing to me when I come home: "There you are!" And often follows with "I love you."

Cosmo may live to be fifty years old. Most African Greys do. She will probably outlast me, unless I live to be a hundred and five, so I have put her into my will. When I take my dirt nap, Cosmo will reside with a wonderful, animal-loving, younger family whom she already knows.

Since I want Cosmo to have a happy life in the future with people who love her, I am working hard to make her lovable and well behaved.

It's annual evaluation time. Let's see what progress Cosmo has made in becoming a lovable and well-behaved bird.

ACHIEVEMENTS:

Excellent talking skills
Clean vocabulary—actually Betty Jean's achievemen
Excellent sense of humorr
Excellent social skills with company
Excellent cuddling and kissing skills
Excellent whistling skills (solos, as well as duets with Betty Jean)
Excellent ability to create fun
Excellent at staying quiet when Betty Jean takes a nap
Excellent at not pooping in cabinets or drawers
Excellent at not pooping on Betty Jean

AREAS REQUIRING IMPROVEMENT:

Biting company's toes and ankles—forbidden
Biting fingers—forbidden
Pooping on floor—frowned upon
Turning base boards into sawdust—forbidden
Getting into Betty Jean's make-up drawer—forbidden
Taking apart pens, lipsticks, eyeliners—forbidden
Destroying books—forbidden

Do you give your pets annual evaluations?

I want Cosmo's future family to want her in the room with them, wherever they may be. Cosmo, like all parrots, will always want to be with her people where the action is.

Parrots have long lives. Generally, the larger the bird, the longer the life. Cosmo is a Congo African grey parrot who weighs sixteen ounces. The other variety of African grey is a Timneh, originating in West Africa. According to The Caged Bird Courier, the greys' lifespan is predicted to be from fifty-to-sixty years.

Macaws, some of them weighing more than three and a half pounds in adulthood, live from fifty to one hundred years. Cockatoos, from forty to sixty years, depending on the variety. Amazons, from fifty to seventy years. Cockatiels, from twelve to twenty. Lovebirds, from fifteen to twenty-five. Budgies, from seven to eighteen.

Inviting a parrot to join your family thus means a lifetime commitment. To be happy, your parrot will need lots of intellectual stimulation, social activity, attention, and love.

Happy parrots make wonderful pets. Unhappy parrots do not. Unhappy, bored, lonely, neglected, or abandoned parrots may pluck out all their feathers. They may bite ferociously. They may scream incessantly, triggering a vicious cycle in which their humans put them in a back room or keep them locked up in a cage and make them even more unhappy, bored, and lonely. How tragic for the parrot.

Cosmo is by all measures a happy parrot.

To make Cosmo attractive for her future family, I make sure she has a clean vocabulary. I don't allow any guests in my house to use foul language, no dirty words, because I don't want Cosmo to pick them up. This is in Cosmo's best interests. She loves to be with me when I have company at home, and she loves to go with me to dinner at the home of friends. I would not allow her out in public if she were not polite. Nor would she get any invitations.

I do have a sense of humor, but I'm rather serious about my house rule against swearing. When Cosmo was just over a year old, she was picking up vocabulary astonishingly fast. My dear brother in El Paso, to amuse me, left a naughty message on my answering machine for Cosmo to hear while I was at work. This was the message: "Hello, Cosmo. Here's a new word for you to learn: Fart."

Yikes! I immediately muted the answering machine. I was not amused.

Cosmo repeated the word a few times before I got her to say "bark" instead.

Several weeks later, when I felt safe, I unmuted the machine. Soon thereafter I heard Cosmo say in my voice, "You have reached 5496243. Beep!"

CHAPTER 10

Empathy

"**W**ANNA GO TO BED Cosmo, okay?"

Cosmo's English was not perfect, but her message was clear.

The problem last night, and every night, was that Cosmo was teasing me. We had been cuddling while I watched Out of Africa. I took Cosmo to her roost cage in her darkened room, but she wouldn't go in. She clutched my hand tightly, sinking her little talons into my fingers, and refused to let go.

We returned to my bedroom, or rather, my dogs' and my bedroom, and I deposited Cosmo atop the cage there. Cosmo greeted the dogs "Woo woo woo!" and whistled a medley of her favorite tunes, told her favorite jokes, mimicked the ringing of the phone, and sent me kisses. She admired herself in the mirror: "That's Cosmo, smooch smooch, whatta bird." She told me again "Cosmo wanna go to bed," and immediately scrambled up the rope perch out of my reach, chuckling.

This went on for thirty minutes. After a while, Cosmo started grinding her beak, which she does when she's contented. She yawned. At last she was sleepy!

I usually have to take Cosmo to bed twice at least. Tired as she may be, she doesn't want to quit the fun she's having with her flock. Nor would I, if I were she.

When she finally lets me carry her to her roost cage, Cosmo hops onto her perch, tucks one foot under her belly, squats down on her other foot to lock her toes in place, sweetly says, "Good night," and closes her eyes.

Since parrots are never off their feet unless they are flying, we parrot-keepers must provide perches of varying diameters to keep our beloved birds from getting arthritis in their feet.

And we must let them get exercise. That means freedom from the cage to walk around.

My heart aches for the unfortunate bird who spends his life in a cage gripping a single perch. Before long the bird will probably become grumpy from arthritic pain. Then his humans won't like him anymore and won't let him out of the cage. And he'll suffer more and get grumpier.

If we compare two pet parrots, an obviously happy one who has had much mental stimulation and an obviously sad one who has had little, we will probably judge the happy one to be considerably more intelligent than the sad one. The two parrots will seem extremely different from each other.

If we compare two wild parrots, we will probably be unable to distinguish them from each other in either intelligence or temperament. They will seem alike to us. Wild parrots share the same exciting natural environment where they forage for food, flee from predators, interact with each other, pair off, and raise their families. They develop similarly.

Nobody is born ill-tempered. Not parrots, not dogs, cats, ostriches, or camels, and not humans. So how do individuals become ill-tempered? Probably stress.

We can do much to alleviate stress on our animals if we imagine what they're thinking.

I propose a game for us humans to play. Let's close our eyes for one minute and imagine being in the mind of one of our pets. Now let's imagine what makes our pet happy and what makes her unhappy. What is worrisome? What is distressing?

I imagine being a six-inch tall parrot, weighing one pound, having feathers, a beak, zygodactyl feet, wings that won't work, eyesight and hearing better than my keeper's, and avian intelligence my keeper can't match. I don't talk because nobody has talked with me. I spend every day stuck in a cage. I imagine waiting hours for somebody to play with me.

Now I imagine being Cosmo, exploring the house, discovering what's in Betty Jean's cabinets and drawers. I imagine having fun with Betty Jean at bedtime, getting her to laugh with me, whistle with me, talk with me, cuddle with me, dance with me, and give me her full attention. I imagine teasing Betty Jean and making her say, "Cosmoooo!" I imagine thinking that being with Betty Jean is what I, Cosmo, a good, good bird, live for.

What if humans empathized with all our fellow inhabitants of Earth—human and non-human? We could figure out how we might be causing each other stress, making each other ill-tempered. Would we want to make each other happier?

Scritches

CHAPTER 11

Poop

BECAUSE OF POPULAR DEMAND, but with apologies to the squeamish, I will discuss poop today. After all, Cosmo discusses poop every day.

Poop was one of the first words she learned.

When she awakens in the morning, Cosmo calls out, "I'm here! Cosmo wanna poop!"

She tells me so that I can let her out of her roost cage in the sunroom and take her to the perch in my bedroom.

After doing her business she proclaims, "Cosmo is a good bird! Cosmo poop on paper!"

Cosmo is not such a good bird when she walks around the house. Fortunately, I have hardwood floors. If she poops near me, she immediately confesses, "Cosmo poop on floor." If she poops out of my sight, she mutters to herself, "Cosmo poop." I hear her, and I hurry to the site with a paper towel and a vinegar-based multi-surface cleanser. As I spray the spot, Cosmo mimics the sound *whiss* and adds, "That's for Cosmo poop!"

When I pick up the roll of paper towels, Cosmo says, "That's paper for Cosmo poop." When I put fresh newspaper on the bottom of a cage," she observes, "That's paper for Cosmo poop in cage." But when I extract the soiled newspaper, she says the same thing: "That's paper for Cosmo poop in cage." Occasionally, she says, "That's paper for cage," or "That's paper for poop."

So Cosmo knows that both the paper towel and the newspaper are dedicated to her poop. That's good reasoning. She knows that the cleanser is dedicated to her poop. She also knows that I am dedicated to cleaning up her poop.

Cosmo thinks a lot about poop. That's probably because, like any bird, she poops a lot. Since parrots metabolize their food much faster than most mammals, parrots usually need to poop every fifteen to thirty minutes.

A parrot's digestive system may seem strange to us mammals. Food goes from the beak through the esophagus to the crop, or craw, where it is moistened and where it can be temporarily stored. From there it goes into the gizzard, where it is ground up, and on to the small intestine, where the nutrients enter the bloodstream. The bird excretes her poop through the same organ, the cloaca, that she uses for mating and egg-laying. It is odorless.

Bird poop has three noticeably different components: feces, which is the solid waste; urates, the pasty white waste produced by the kidneys; and urine, the liquid waste produced by the kidneys.

We can learn what a parrot has eaten by observing the color of her feces. If Cosmo has been eating primarily pellets, as would be ideal, her feces will be brown. If she has been eating carrots, squash, or sweet potatoes, all of which she likes, her feces will have an orange hue. If she has been eating spinach or other greens, her feces will be green. Naturally. The urates remain white and the urine clear.

African grey parrots in the wild will not defecate where they roost at night, for their poop can attract predators. That is why Cosmo asks to get out of her cage as soon as she awakens. She wants to do her morning poop away from where she sleeps.

Some parrot owners claim that they have potty-trained their birds. I was skeptical until I met Scott Gold, Professor of Plant Pathology at the University of Georgia. Scott is famous in Athens for teaching class with his peach-faced lovebird Georgio under his shirt. Georgio, like his predecessor Angelino, poops only when Scott invites him to poop in a suitable location—into a paper napkin, for instance.

Cosmo is not potty-trained, but she doesn't poop on me.

In the evenings, before I put her into her roost cage to go to sleep, she asks to cuddle.

"Betty Jean wanna cuddle?" I do. We cuddle for fifteen or twenty minutes.

Cosmo obviously feels pleasure from the scritches I give her. "Scritches," as most parrot lovers know, are the gentle wrong-way caresses we give our birds on their head and neck where they can't preen themselves.

After a while she says, "Cosmo wanna poop." I place her on her T-stand and she poops.

Cosmo has figured out that the word *poop* is funny, especially to young humans. When Cosmo and I visit elementary schools, I tell the children about Cosmo's learning to talk. Cosmo listens attentively, because she recognizes many of my words. She knows that I am talking about her.

After a while, she says, "Cosmo wanna poop." The children laugh. Cosmo repeats the word, this time louder, "Poop!" The children laugh some more. Cosmo laughs, and then says it again and again, "Poop! Cosmo gonna poop!" Then she poops.

The children roar with laughter. So does Cosmo.

CHAPTER 12

Learning

WHEN SHE WAS YOUNG, between one and two years of age, Cosmo would practice her English early in the morning. She would say many words quietly to herself before summoning me to her cage with her usual morning call: "I'm here!"

Now Cosmo talks to herself for her own amusement. I eavesdrop to learn what she's thinking about. It's doggies, birdies, squirrel, herself, where everybody is, what she's gonna do, where Betty Jean gonna go, what she wants to eat, etc., interspersed with whistles, telephone rings, dog barks, bird calls, other environmental sounds, and laughter when she says something she knows is funny. She laughs at her own jokes.

I got what I had wished for—infinitely more than I had wished for—when I brought Cosmo home. I have been able to peek into the thoughts of a non-human animal because she gives voice to her thoughts in my language. I don't know what squirrels and crows think, because they don't let me know.

But after living with Cosmo, I know that squirrels and crows do think.

Many animal lovers have read the book *Alex and Me*, in which Irene Pepperberg tells of her male African grey parrot's intellectual achievements. By the time he died at the age of thirty-one, Alex could identify in English fifty different objects, seven colors, five shapes, and quantities up to six. He had developed a sense of humor and the ability to deceive. He had combined words to make novel, meaningful utterances. For example, he called cake "yummy bread." He had many of the social skills that Cosmo has acquired plus the rudiments of a first-grade education.

Pepperberg's research on Alex, collected in *The Alex*

Studies, broke ground in the field of animal cognition and proved that African greys, and probably many other birds, had mental abilities far beyond our previous expectations. Irene Pepperberg did for our understanding of parrots what Jane Goodall did for our understanding of primates.

But I've been thinking about the evidence Pepperberg used to prove Alex's intelligence. Why did Pepperberg feel obliged to teach Alex colors and numbers to demonstrate his intelligence? Why would a bird need to count to convince humans that he was intelligent?

Why would a bird ever need to count? Would an African grey in the Congo think: "I hear my mate calling. She is behind the third bush on the left?"

I am reluctant to use any single scale to measure the intelligence of different animals. Or of different humans, for that matter. When humans—whether we're teachers, anthropologists, or animal behaviorists—measure the abilities of beings unlike us, we inevitably measure them against our own, presumably superior, abilities.

Those of us who have been teachers know that the tests we give our human students measure what they've learned for the tests and not their creativity, their resourcefulness, their ability to escape predators, or their sense of direction. The tests don't measure who they are.

If we try to assess the intelligence of Cosmo, we must keep in mind that she does all her talking in a language foreign to her species. Imagine having your intelligence judged on the basis of what you discuss in first-year Japanese.

Cosmo does all her thinking in an environment foreign to her species—my house. I venture to say that Alex had far greater mental abilities than he could show by identifying fifty different objects and counting up to six. Those achievements were simply answers to the researchers' test questions.

What researchers cannot measure by human standards is a Canada goose's ability to follow the same migration patterns every year, a foxhound's ability to visualize who preceded him on a trail, a Pacific salmon's ability to return to her freshwater birthplace to spawn and die after years of living in the ocean.

If we divide abilities into the categories of intellectual and instinctual, call our human abilities intellectual, and then rank them higher than other animals' so-called instinctual abilities, we fail to appreciate the glorious mental power of all the world's inhabitants.

I love living with Cosmo. We talk with each other, laugh together at her jokes, and whistle duets. She teases me, I cuddle her, we "go in a car," we "have company," we share coconut ice cream.

After she tells me, "Cosmo wanna go to bed," and I put her in her roost cage and close the door to her darkened room, I think in awe of what my feathery, sixteen-ounce companion has accomplished to be such a "good good bird" in my world.

CHAPTER 13

A Beak

COSMO IS SO BAD! I don't know why I still love her.

Last night while I was clearing off the dining room table after dinner, Cosmo climbed into the open dishwasher and removed—without breaking—the plastic fastener that held the upper tray in place. Rattle clatter boom bang. All the glasses shifted position, and the upper tray smashed into the dishes beneath.

The crash caught my attention. I rushed over. There was Cosmo, holding the intact fastener in her right foot and lifting it to her beak. She has excellent beak-foot coordination.

"Cosmooooooooo!" I cried at the top of my lungs.

"Cosmooo-ooo-ooo!" she echoed mockingly.

I persuaded Cosmo to step onto my hand and relinquish the fastener. I tried to put the fastener back but got it all wrong, so the next day I asked my smart neighbor Jim to come fix it. He did. Jim can fix anything from dishwashers to snakes.

How embarrassing! Not that a man is more mechanically savvy than I am—I'm used to that—but a bird?

I'm interested in Cosmo's beak because I don't have one. So I looked up parrot beaks on the web.

All parrots have a pointed, hooked beak. That's why breeders call parrots hookbills. The larger parrots with the most powerful beaks like the macaws, amazons, and cockatoos are capable of cracking the shells of nuts, tearing open thick-skinned fruit, grinding tough seeds, and defending themselves against predators. A Hyacinth macaw can crush a brazil nut with a force of one thousand pounds per square inch. A blue and gold macaw can crush a macadamia nut. Cosmo can crack open an almond. Obviously, if they tried, all these

Cosmo explores the dishwasher.

parrots could do serious damage to one's finger or one's lip.

But hookbills also use their beaks like a third hand, with dexterity and sensitivity. In fact, their hooked beak differentiates parrots from non-parrots, as do their zygodactyl feet and their human-like ability to bring their foot to their beak when eating. No other bird can eat like that.

By the way, African greys and most other parrots—as well as woodpeckers and owls—have zygodactyl feet. The first and fourth toes face backwards, and the second and third toes face forward. This arrangement is as useful to birds as an opposable thumb is to us primates. Cosmo can pick up anything she wants to eat, investigate, or destroy.

Parrots are unique in another way. They can move their upper mandible independently from their lower mandible and from their head. That physical ability enables parrots to manipulate objects—and disassemble pens and locks and dishwasher fasteners—with great dexterity.

Cosmo uses her beak to extract peas from peapods leaving the peapod in one piece, to pry open walnuts, to yank open drawers and cabinet doors, to unscrew locks in her cage, to take apart necklace clasps, to groom herself and me, to peel fruit, to climb, and to eat.

Cosmo also uses her beak to shape sound into words.

And Cosmo uses her beak to kiss me. Of course. I notice when she gives me a kiss that her beak is warm. That's because it has blood vessels and nerve endings inside.

It's not just her superb coordination of hooked beak, zygodactyl feet, and sharper-than-human eyesight that enables Cosmo to disassemble gadgets. It's her brain. Cosmo encountered the tray fastener during her exploration of the dishwasher, discovered how to unlock it, and then removed the fastener with her beak. What fun! She must have loved the intellectual challenge. She had to work fast before I'd spy her where she wasn't supposed to be.

What I find interesting is that Cosmo could have cracked the fastener and crushed it but did not. Instead she opened it.

Cosmo does the same with pens, eyeliners, and lipsticks. She opens them. She does not crush them.

But she crushes, shreds, and grinds almost everything else.

Cosmo often looks at herself in the mirror, pecks the mirror with her beak, and says, "That's Cosmo. Cosmo has a beak" or just "That's Cosmo has a beak."

Cosmo became curious about my teeth one morning when she was perching on the towel rack by the sink watching me brush. "What's that?" she asked.

I didn't know whether she was referring to my toothbrush or my teeth, so I pointed to my teeth and said, "That's teeth. Betty Jean has teeth. Cosmo has a beak."

Cosmo leaned toward me to get a better look. I opened my mouth. She peered in. She tapped my front tooth with her beak. Then she tapped a couple of others.

Now when she kisses me, she wants to check out my teeth. I let her.

While I've been writing, Cosmo has been on her perch behind me grinding her beak, moving her mandibles from side to side. That's a sign of contentment. She's tucked one foot up under her belly. She's about to fall asleep.

She looks innocent

Cosmo at dinner. *Photo by Susan Tate*

CHAPTER 14

Language's Categories

NOT LONG AGO I took Cosmo to see one of the fine veterinarians at Hope Animal Medical Center. I don't want my precious parrot to fly into a window or through a door, so we go there twice a year for flight-feather clipping and a general physical. The visit gave me lots of food for thought.

After the technician had carried Cosmo into the recesses of the building to work on her, I heard riotous laughter. I waited and waited for the technician to return Cosmo to me. Then more laughter, giggles, and chuckles. It seemed like the whole staff was having a party in the back.

Finally, Dr. Stacy emerged with Cosmo and a report on Cosmo's anti-authoritarian behavior. Apparently Cosmo had refused to leave her cage. When Dr. Stacy opened the cage door, Cosmo climbed every which way but out to avoid capture. When the humans laughed, Cosmo laughed, and then everybody fell to giggling. Cosmo amused herself further.

Dr. Stacy removed the cage top in the expectation that Cosmo would climb up. Instead, Cosmo flipped backwards on the rope perch, went limp, and hung upside down from one foot, out of reach. Cosmo chuckled, and so did everybody else.

The report probably went into Cosmo's permanent record.

Years ago when she visited the clinic for a nail trim, Cosmo looked up out of the towel in which the vet had wrapped her and said pitifully, "Cosmo wanna be a good bird!" She did not have fun.

This time Cosmo had more fun. She met a cat named Creamsicle. As soon as I carried Cosmo's cage with Cosmo inside into the waiting room, curious Creamsicle approached Cosmo to look her over. Cosmo showed great interest in

Creamsicle and barked softly. "Woo woo woo."

Although she was simply greeting Creamsicle, Cosmo startled the little cat, who immediately backed away from the cage. Probably Creamsicle had never seen a bird who barked.

At first I thought that Cosmo was playing with Creamsicle, treating her like a dog. But then I realized that Cosmo had never seen a cat. Cosmo had learned only three words for the animals in her life: "dog," "bird," and "squirrel" and their variations, "doggies," "birdies," and "squirrelies." She had to fit any animal she encountered into one of those categories.

Cosmo has seen dogs of all kinds and sizes, from a Pekingese named Oscar to a Labrador-retriever mix named Shane and a Labradoodle named Annie Hall. She calls them all doggies. She has seen many varieties of birds, from chickadees to woodpeckers and crows. She has seen squirrels and chipmunks. She has seen humans, whom I guess she categorizes as "company." If she has a separate category for me, she has not disclosed it.

Cosmo fitted Creamsicle into the category of "dog." Creamsicle had fur, whiskers, and a tail, like every dog she knew.

If Cosmo saw a pig, I presume she'd say, "That's doggie." I might have my feelings hurt if she said, "That's company."

Years ago I started thinking about how we humans structure reality through our language. I had read the book Language, Thought, and Reality in which 1930s linguist Benjamin Lee Whorf wrote that Hopi grammar and vocabulary inclined the Hopi Indians to organize their experiences differently from English speakers. Whorf argued that all humans think within language and that our particular language affects the possibilities and limitations of our thought. In other words, our language sets up categories into which we fit what we encounter.

Whorf did not persuade all linguists to his way of thinking, but he persuaded me. I considered his theory applicable not only to humans but also to non-human users of language such as Koko the gorilla, who communicated to humans through

American Sign Language.

When Cosmo learned to talk, I assumed that her acquaintance with English, however simplified, was influencing her to view the world differently from the way she would have viewed it had she not acquired speech. English gave her conceptual categories, as it does to all language speakers. However, most English-speaking humans have more conceptual categories than Cosmo does.

Do other animals—those trillions who don't speak to us humans—have conceptual categories to make sense of their experiences? The categories of predator, prey, danger, food, water, mate, babies, family, and perhaps friend?

There's no way of finding out, unfortunately, because as soon as we give an animal the language that would let him tell us, we've given him our categories.

After realizing that Cosmo must categorize all foods as "peanut," "grape," or "corn," and all animals as "dog," bird," or "squirrel," I see that my access to her thoughts is as limited as the grammar and vocabulary I gave her. She knows in her bird brain that pork and pineapple are different from each other, but to request a bite she must use the vocabulary she has.

At the veterinary clinic, did Cosmo not recognize any significant difference between Creamsicle and the dogs she's met? I can't answer that, and Cosmo can't tell me.

But Cosmo has taught me something very important: that communication of thoughts and feelings in language is not a measure of those thoughts and feelings—not in anybody, whether feathery, furry, or hairy.

Cosmo has also taught me. Communication with individuals of any species, however it happens, can bring pleasure.

When Cosmo barked "woo woo woo" to Creamsicle, she was trying to communicate with her. Cosmo wanted to make friends.

CHAPTER 15

Parrot Trade

MY DEAR LITTLE COSMO has made me a better person than I was before she first stepped trustingly onto my hand. I'm convinced. She's made me more sensitive to the thoughts and feelings of all the uncaged birds in my neighborhood and all the other animals on our planet. She's made me more concerned about how we humans treat the animals we eat. And she's made me more distressed about the pet trade.

Cosmo is perched behind me on her T-stand as I write. She just asked, "How are you?"

I said, "Fine, thank you. How are you?"

Cosmo said, "Fine, thank you. How are you?"

I got up, kissed her, and sat back down to write this essay.

Cosmo went over to her food dish, picked up a raw, unsalted cashew, flung it across the room, and laughed. I'm going to ignore that.

I am amazed by Cosmo's intelligence and her adaptability to my household but I am even more impressed by the depth of her emotions. When Cosmo asks to cuddle she means it. She puts her head against my chest and closes her eyes in anticipation of the caresses she will get. She wants to cuddle every night before going to sleep.

Are parrots in the wild this affectionate to each other? This sensitive? If so, what terror must they experience when they are captured? What sorrow must they feel when they are confined to an aviary, with their memories of life in the rain forest?

Cosmo's ancestors were caught in the central African rainforests and sent to an aviary, maybe the one in Florida where Cosmo was hatched. Her parents didn't get to choose their spouse as did their more fortunate un-caught relatives. Instead, they had to marry the bird their breeders selected for them. And although their instincts told them they should keep their family together for a year or two, they were forced to give up Cosmo and her clutch mates after four months, long before they'd finished feeding them, teaching them their chirps, or educating them in the ways of Congo African greys.

I find myself in an ethical conflict-of-interest position. I bought Cosmo to be my pet. But I am opposed to the capture and trade of wild parrots and disturbed by the breeding of birds for the pet trade.

I have been asked how I justify keeping an African grey as a pet. After all, I would not have Cosmo if ruthless pet traders had not captured her unlucky ancestors in the Congo and sold them to breeders in the United States.

I have heard arguments against keeping parrots as pets. But if one treats the bird as a sensitive individual in need of affection, exercise, mental stimulation, and freedom from cage, I would defend bringing a parrot into one's family as much as I would a dog or a cat. We humans learn from our pets. Our empathy with a bird in hand leads to our empathy with many birds in the bush.

Cosmo's family history does disturb me. I am glad that the trade of wild-caught African greys is now against international law, even if the legislation's rationa   le is to sustain their population in the wild. Whatever the reason may be for the legal protection of animals—whether it is conservation of species, preservation of biodiversity, or prevention of cruelty to individuals—I'm for it.

Cosmo was hatched in a breeder's aviary. And she turned out to be a smart, happy, home-loving bird. But she could easily have turned out otherwise.

Deb Allwein, who operates the parrot sanctuary No-R-Birds in Nicholson, Georgia, reminds us that aviculturists these days do not breed parrots for temperament or adaptability to human society. They breed them for brilliantly colored feathers, because buyers want beauty.

We buyers need to reassess our values. Brilliantly colored feathers do not necessarily make for marvelous companions. Or happy caged birds, for that matter.

The words "happy" and "caged" do not go together.

Parrots are not decorations for the living room. They are feathery persons with thoughts and feelings who are capable of immeasurable sadness and consequent anger. If we would not confine a handsome dog to a gilded cage in the living room, why would we confine a parrot?

"Because a parrot poops," you reply. Well, I'll be darned. You're right. Live birds poop. But should pooping be punished by a life sentence in a cage?

According to the World Parrot Trust, African Greys have been among the most internationally traded wild birds for fifty years. Twenty-one percent of their global population is captured every year.

In 1992 Congress passed the Wild Bird Conservation Act, which bans the importation into the United States of most wild birds on the CITES lists of endangered species. African greys are on that list.

CITES, which stands for the Convention on International Trade in Endangered Species of Wild Fauna and Flora, is an agreement signed in 1973 by eighty countries to "ensure that international trade in specimens of wild animals and plants does not threaten their survival."

Although the legislation's intention is to prevent extinction, it functions to protect individuals as well. However, the very legislation that protects the parrots creates a lucrative black market for them.

The wild-caught trade flourishes because African grey parrots do not start reproducing until they are six years old. Unscrupulous breeders prefer to buy wild-caught, already mature birds to avoid the costs of raising them to reproductive age. They can buy one thousand parrots for a hundred thousand dollars and then sell their offspring for much, much more.

Thus thousands of these intelligent animals are smuggled

across borders every year, sometimes with horrifying disregard for the birds' wellbeing. For example, in 2010, Cameroon law enforcers discovered a shipment of more than a thousand wild-caught African Greys stuffed into tiny crates scheduled to be transported to the Middle East on an Ethiopian plane. Wallowing in their own waste and having been deprived of food and water, many of the frightened birds were injured and in need of immediate medical care. Cameroon's Limbe Wildlife Center took the birds in, treated them, and released them into the wild.

What was each bird thinking all this while?

Chapter 16

Intelligence

AFTER DINNER TONIGHT Cosmo wiped her beak on my sleeve, leaving peanut butter on my blouse. I had picked her up after she'd enjoyed her favorite messy meal and she used my sleeve as her personal napkin. Oh, well. After eating Cosmo always wipes her beak clean, usually on a rope but sometimes on me.

Now she's perched on my chair behind me. I'm watching Little Miss Sunshine, or rather, trying to watch that movie. Here's part of the conversation we've been having.

> Cosmo: "Cosmo is a good bird. Do you wanna kiss? Smooch!"
> Betty Jean: "Smooch! I love you."
> Cosmo: "What's that?"
> Betty Jean: "That's television."
> Cosmo: "Rrring rrring rrring. You have reached 5496243. Telephone for Betty Jean."
> Betty Jean: "Hello."
> Cosmo: "Hi. How are you? Wanna go for a walk? Okay. Thank you. Good-bye. Beep."
> Betty Jean: "Good-bye."
> Cosmo: "You have reached 549.... Telephone for bird! Hahaha!"

I've presented this transcript not to show how smart Cosmo is but to show how playful she is, how well she has adapted to her environment, and how much fun we have with each other. Although Cosmo seems highly intelligent, I don't claim that she's smarter than your dog, who has probably also adapted well to his environment.

I looked up intelligence on Wikipedia and found this definition: the capability of "abstract thought, understanding, self-awareness, communication, reasoning, learning, having emotional knowledge, retaining, planning, and problem solving." Wow. That describes humans!

However, these days we're discovering that many non-human animals are also communicative and intelligent, even according to our human-centric definition of intelligence. In fact, many more individuals than we once imagined communicate with each other within their flock, pod, colony, whatever. I'm thinking of parrots, dolphins, whales, and a whole lot of other birds and mammals who communicate by transmission of sound. And then there are ants, who communicate by transmission of scent. Seems like everybody communicates by signals of one sort or another.

If I were Definer-in-Chief of The Dictionary, I'd describe intelligence as the ability to employ one's senses to obtain valuable awareness and understanding of one's physical and social environment, combined with the ability to modify one's behavior quickly in response to the demands and opportunities of the situation.

We could apply this definition to all animals, including humans. We could determine who is the most intelligent member of a pack of dogs, herd of boar, murder of crows, band of jays, bevy of quail, exaltation of larks, pride of lions, gaggle of geese, tribe of monkeys, bloat of hippopotamuses, school of cod, fever of stingrays, smack of jellyfish, shiver of sharks, mess of iguanas, army of caterpillars, and troop of boy scouts.

However, if we're not deciding whom to admit to college, why would we need to?

If I were young, I'd want to study animal behavior and cognition. I'd be interested in discovering how non-human animals play, learn, perceive the world, communicate with each other, and interact with individuals of different species. But I'd not be interested in ranking them according to their intelligence, either within species or among species, because their intelligence should not determine how we humans treat them.

Now I'm probably most curious about the interaction of individuals of different species in play. Such interaction shows the ability to take advantage of an unusual situation. That's intelligence, as I see it. Here's an example.

A few days ago my little dog Mary wanted to play. She can no longer play with my dog Kaylee, because Kaylee's old and bored with Mary's antics, so Mary resorts to playing with me, and with Cosmo.

Mary jumped onto the bed, lowered her head to her paws, stuck her rear end in the air in typical doggy-play fashion, made eye contact with me, and then lunged at me and jumped back. All you dog lovers can picture her. Cosmo happened to be on my left hand when Mary initiated the game, and whenever Mary lowered her head, I lowered mine, to bed level, and Cosmo lowered hers and stuck her tail feathers in the air. I'd try to touch Mary's paw, and Mary would jump back. Then she'd lunge, and I would straighten up. So would Cosmo. Then Mary, Cosmo, and I would lower our heads once more and repeat the confrontation.

That form of play is instinctive to dogs.

But not to parrots. To parrots it is learned.

Does it show "the ability to modify one's behavior quickly in response to the demands and opportunities of the situation?" Of course it does. It shows Cosmo's intelligence.

Chapter 17

Preening

YESTERDAY SOME NEIGHBORS came over for wine and tapas. After saying "Hello," Cosmo turned her attention to personal upkeep. She preened while she listened to our conversation, chiming in only when she heard her name uttered.

Cosmo spends much of the day preening, and much of the evening having me preen her. Only I don't do oil gland work.

All parrots, and most birds, preen. They do it when they are happy and comfortable with their surroundings. It makes them feel good, and it makes them attractive to their mates.

Cosmo has some eight thousand feathers to keep beautiful. Occasionally, she has a bad feather day, when a feather sticks out, but she promptly remedies the cosmetic problem. Preening involves conditioning and waterproofing the feathers. With her beak Cosmo extracts oil from the heart-shaped uropygial gland at the base of her tail and then meticulously applies the oil to each feather.

She removes the tough sheaths from emerging feathers.

And she checks her body for mites. I'm delighted to tell you that she doesn't have any. Neither do I.

I still thrill to watch my self-confident avian friend take such excellent care of herself.

After preening for a while, Cosmo will stretch. She'll extend her wings and spread her tail feathers. Then she'll ruffle her body feathers and go all fluffy.

I'll say, "Wow! Whatta bird!"

Cosmo will usually wiggle her tail in appreciation of my compliment and begin a conversation. "Cosmo has feathers. Cosmo is a good good bird!"

Cosmo is a neatnik. Not only does she clean her feathers

but she also cleans her beak after eating, and after kissing me. Cosmo can't tolerate lipstick, pieces of corn, or drops of orange juice on her beak, so she rubs her beak on the rope to get rid of anything sticking to it.

I'm glad to say that Cosmo's desire for cleanliness does not override her desire for another kiss.

"Betty Jean wanna kiss?" she'll ask out of the blue after twenty minutes of preening quietly. I give her a kiss.

If Cosmo had a spouse, she and her spouse would allopreen, or preen each other. But she doesn't. She's got me. And under Georgia law, we can't be spouses.

However, we can preen each other. Sometimes at night I'll watch a movie with Cosmo perched on the back of my chair grooming herself. Occasionally, I'll feel her poke around in my hair and yank a strand or two.

"Cosmo wanna cuddle," she'll tell me.

"Okay," I tell her. Yes, yes, yes, I think. I prefer cuddling with Cosmo to having her pull my hair, bite my ear, and yank off my glasses, all signs of her affection for me.

Since Cosmo can't tend to her own head, I do it for her. I give her head a gentle "skritching," rubbing the tiny feathers the wrong way to loosen the sheaths around the new ones. I kiss her back whenever she says, "Cosmo wanna kiss feathers," and I caress her neck and shoulders. Cosmo closes her eyes in delight.

African greys exude a whitish powder. When I hold Cosmo on my lap, my clothes get dusty, revealing to any unexpected visitors that Cosmo and I have been cuddling. Fine by me.

Last night while preening, Cosmo was apparently paying close attention to my movie, *Blow Out*. In the movie, an owl hooted, and Cosmo immediately announced, "That's a birdy." A phone rang, and Cosmo answered, in a voice just like mine, "Hello?" The owl hooted again, and Cosmo said again, "That's a birdy."

Cosmo was discussing the movie with me while she was doing her feathers. I was doing my nails. We preened together.

CHAPTER 18

Community of Life

COSMO JUST BECKONED ME. "Look, birdy, squirrel!" She was standing on the floor by the sliding glass door of the sunroom watching two chipmunks, three squirrels, six or seven doves, and a male cardinal all eating together on the deck. They are my outdoor guests and Cosmo's. They're wild.

Cosmo and my dogs Kaylee and Mary are my indoor guests. They're tame.

The flying squirrels who inhabit my attic are my uninvited guests who are capable of living outside but prefer to make their home in my house. They're wild, or wildish.

Apparently, I have other seldom seen guests. Raccoons and possums wait until dark to claim a share of the seeds, peanuts, and corn that I put out for the daytime guests; and the Eastern woodrats live under my deck and enjoy the leftovers.

My wildlife removal man advised that for three weeks I refrain from feeding my outdoor guests while he trapped the residents of my attic. I declined his advice because I didn't want to disappoint my furry and feathery dependents. What would they do without me?

I suspect my naturalist friends would say they'd do just fine.

Cosmo is an avid bird and squirrel watcher. So I want to attract wildlife here. Or wildish-life. I don't offer bear chow.

We Americans love having wildlife in our neighborhoods. We select the animals we want to have as our visitors, and then we lay out a buffet customized to their tastes. They are part of our exterior decor. Like the grill.

As realtors come to recognize what buyers want, they'll put ads in the paper that say, for example, "Cedar house on wooded lot with two bedrooms, two baths, hummingbirds, cardinals, mourning doves, finches, chickadees, owls, chipmunks, and red oaks. Close to elementary school, grocery stores, and restaurants."

They probably won't place an ad that says, "Cedar house on wooded lot with two bedrooms, two baths, flying squirrels, gray squirrels, carpenter bees, bats, raccoons, possums, armadillos, deer, mice, wood rats, rat snakes, slugs, snails, and poison ivy. Close to elementary school, grocery stores, and restaurants."

Actually, I'm talking about my house. I sought professional help to get rid of the undesirables. No problem, I thought. Good-bye, flying squirrels, carpenter bees, rat snakes, poison ivy. So long, slugs. *Adiós, ratas. Adieu, escargots.*

However, complications developed. I wanted to keep the owls, but I'd removed the wood rats and flying squirrels, whom the owls would have eaten for dinner. So the owls left. I got rid of the rat snakes, who would have eaten the wood rats. So the wood rats returned.

I sprayed the slugs—who are hermaphrodites, by the way—with slug-icide and sent them to Slug Heaven. Then I learned that slugs eat raccoon droppings, which my dogs like to roll in. Furthermore, slugs are food for birds, whom I want to keep around. Without the slugs, the birds will become even more dependent on me.

I'll need to buy more seeds for the birds, because I've gotten the system out of whack. Good gracious! Seems like every decision I make has side effects. Help!

Oh, rat snakes, will you ever return? I apologize for discombobulating your community.

I think the real estate ad should say: "Woodsy community surrounding cedar house with two bedrooms, two baths." Then the buyer will know that she's joining a community of life, and not simply moving into a stand-alone house to which she may invite a few well-behaved, attractive wildish animals.

When we tinker with one thing, we unintentionally change everything. Humans see only parts of the community, but the community of life is greater than the sum of its parts. It's animated by all the individual organisms engaged in work that affects each other.

In nature nothing stands alone. Everything is joined to something else.

Cosmo has some traits I like and some I don't. She talks, tells jokes, laughs, makes me laugh, mimics every sound she hears, reads my mind, and loves me. She also poops on the floor, chews the baseboards, chases the dogs, and bites.

However, I've learned that the traits I like and the traits I don't are all part of the whole wonderful system that is Cosmo. I can't change one thing without changing another.

Cosmo is not my creation. She is nature's. She's a product of evolution. Cosmo's doing her best to adapt to a community of life very different from the one a thousand generations of her ancestors enjoyed.

I'm doing my best to adapt to a community that includes her.

CHAPTER 19

Desire to Learn

COSMO HAS BEEN MAKING some grammatical mistakes lately. I must admit, however, her grammar was not perfect before. But neither was the English I employed for our conversations.

Cosmo's been saying, "Cosmo wanna be cuddle." And "Cosmo wanna be kiss." And "Cosmo wanna be go in a car."

Cosmo has long expressed her wishes with the phrase "Cosmo wanna," as in "Cosmo wanna cuddle," "Cosmo wanna kiss," and "Cosmo wanna go in a car." Yet she has said "Cosmo wanna be a good bird" so often—and, on occasion, "Cosmo don't wanna be a good bird"—that she has started substituting "wanna be" for "wanna."

Now Cosmo wanders around the house muttering, "Cosmo wanna be...," whereas she used to mutter, "Cosmo wanna...." She's pretty focused on what she'd like for herself.

Cosmo's speech has evolved in other ways. Yesterday she said, "I don't kiss feathers." I'm sure she meant "I don't wanna kiss feathers." I had said, "Betty Jean wanna kiss feathers." She usually loves to have me kiss her feathers, but yesterday she was demonstrating her independence.

Today, when she entered my study, she asked, "Where are Cosmo?" She was extrapolating from "Where are you?"

These mistakes show that she knows what she's talking about.

As has happened in the past when she has strayed from what she's learned, or has gotten lazy in her pronunciation, if I correct her by saying, for example, "Cosmo wanna cuddle," she'll say it right again. Cosmo likes to learn.

This morning, from atop her cage behind me, Cosmo asked, "Betty Jean wanna whi-hul?" Then she whistled the first bars of a tune she had not whistled for a while, "Heigh-Ho," and listened attentively while I completed it. She repeated it, imperfectly but enthusiastically.

A minute later Cosmo started another tune familiar to her, "Wooden Heart." She whistled a few bars, waited for me to complete it, and promptly whistled the whole thing herself, from beginning to end, a couple of times.

A year ago on the Fourth of July, I whistled "Yankee Doodle." Cosmo stopped preening and gave me all her attention. So I whistled the tune again, and again. Minutes later, Cosmo was whistling parts of it and then waiting for me to fill in. Soon she was whistling the tune, imperfectly but enthusiastically.

Cosmo has asked for help in remembering a tune before. She must consider me her teacher.

Cosmo also composes her own unique melodies, melodies she's never heard me whistle, melodies she could not repeat, long songs lasting perhaps a minute. She whistles them exuberantly. And after she concludes, she exclaims, "Wow!"

Cosmo knows the difference between my melodies and hers. Mine are supposed to be always the same, maybe like bird calls but longer. Hers don't have to be. They can be new and different.

Cosmo doesn't ask for help when she's creating something new and different.

Unlike literate humans, Cosmo doesn't have a written text or a CD recording to aid her memory. She has only me. She has to remembereverything associated with whistling my tunes and speaking my language, the melodies; the sound of the words; their meanings. Naturally, her speaking and whistling evolve over time, unless I continually remind her of the right way—that is, my way—to speak and to whistle.

I find amazing not only the skills Cosmo has that her wild cousins don't have and don't need, but also her conscientiousness in acquiring the skills. When she is trying to learn something, she stands very still and eyes me intently. The pupils of her eyes contract and expand, indicating the intensity of her concentration. That's called "pinpointing" or "flashing."

Is Cosmo studying? The *American Heritage Dictionary* defines *study* as "the effort to acquire knowledge." I'd say that's what Cosmo is doing. She obviously has an inquiring mind. She wants to participate in my speech-filled, whistle-filled world. She wants to acquire my culture.

Cosmo is a sixteen-ounce, six-inch-tall, feathery intellectual.

Now Cosmo is perched on the cage in my bedroom practicing the number four, which she thinks means "many." She just said, "Smooch, smooch, smooch. That's four kiss."

CHAPTER 20

Adaptation

COSMO WATCHED ME as I opened a cardboard box and unpacked a paper shredder.

"What's that?" she asked.

"That's a box," I replied. "Box for Cosmo." I set the box on the floor for her.

Cosmo immediately descended from her perch to begin shredding the box. She concentrated on the task for some fifteen minutes.

Cosmo then tired of the box and headed down the hall. She can't fly so she walks, or rather waddles. Her gait is adorable to me but unnatural for her because she's a bird.

I asked, "Cosmo, where wanna go?"

She said, "Cosmo wanna go to Betty Jean's bedroom." And off she went to be with the dogs.

In the African rain forests, Cosmo's relatives go wherever they like. They fly. They live in large flocks of their own kind. They crack palm nuts.

I can easily see what abilities I've helped Cosmo develop: meaningful speech and a sense of humor. I wonder what abilities I've suppressed in her, besides flying. And mating. And raising a family. And teaching her young their unique parrot names. Dear me.

But Cosmo has adapted quite happily to her unnatural environment. Remember Shania Twayne's song, "Dance with the one that brought you"? Cosmo exemplifies the song's wisdom. She's making a good life for herself with two dogs and a human for a flock, in a house that's not a rain forest.

And she does dance with the one that bought her.

We're all adaptable creatures, humans and Earth's other

residents. That's how we survive as individuals, and that's how we survive as species. Those folks who do not adapt to their environment and do not reproduce do not pass on their genes, obviously. They disappear forever into our planet's past.

Last April I came across a nest that had fallen from some exterior steel rafters of the Wildlife Health Building at the Vet School. According to my friend John Fischer, a University of Georgia wildlife biologist, the nest had belonged to an Eastern phoebe. The phoebe lived in Athen. She was a city bird so she made her nest midst bricks and mortar.

I took the nest home to put on my coffee table. I hoped a guest would see it there and exclaim, "That's a nest!" And then I could reply, "What? Oh, no! How did it get in here?"

While arranging the centerpiece for the coffee table, I looked at the nest. It was basically a cup made of mud, moss, twigs, and grass. A standard phoebe nest. But up close I saw something unusual woven into it. There were fragments of a green net plastic bag, the kind that holds lemons or limes in a grocery store's produce department. Some human had tossed out the plastic, and the resourceful Mrs. Phoebe recognized its potential as construction material. Wow. That's thinking outside the box!

How nice. The phoebe uses what humans discard. Animals make nests in buildings that belong to humans. And humans make houses in woods that belong—or once belonged—to animals. Humans put bird nests on coffee tables. We use each other's stuff. We share. We are family

But wait. We wouldn't put a green net plastic bag in a crib, because the baby could get entangled in it. Should we leave it out for Mrs. Phoebe to put into her nest?

If we are all—humans and other animals—in this together, if we share our stuff, live in each other's space, drink the same water and breathe the same air, have similar brains and comparable feelings, then we probably experience the same health threats.

As I've mentioned before, Cosmo punctuates the highly

original medleys she whistles with trucks' back-up alarms. She too is a city bird, making music out of what she hears in her environment, shredding boxes instead of branches, speaking English instead of whatever meaningful chirps her parrot parents would have taught her if they'd lived together in the rain forest.

When I listen to Cosmo, I hear what my environment sounds like to a bird. I may not have noticed the back-up alarms before, but now I do. And when I look at Mrs. Phoebe's nest, I see what my environment looks like to a bird. I may not have noticed the green net plastic bags at the side of the road, but now I do.

The green net plastic bags now belong to everybody. So do the back-up alarms.

CHAPTER 21

Teasing

I THINK COSMO WAS HATCHED with a sense of humor. When she was seven or eight months old, before she could talk, Cosmo watched me roast green chili peppers in the oven, as I had learned to do in my long-vanished youth in El Paso. As the peppers blackened, their marvelous aroma filled the kitchen. Then the smoke billowing out of the oven set off the smoke alarm. Veeeep. I rushed around turning on fans and opening doors and windows. The smoke alarm stopped.

Apparently, Cosmo noticed.

Two months later, I roasted chili peppers again. Just as they began to smell really good, I heard the smoke alarm. Veeeep. Oh, no! In a panic I hurriedly turned on the fans and opened the doors and windows. But there was no smoke. I looked at the alarm on the wall, near Cosmo's perch. The alarm stopped. I turned back to the oven. The alarm started. Veeeep. I looked up. It stopped. So I disconnected it from the wall and placed it on the counter across the room. But as I did so I heard one more veeeep. It came from Cosmo.

Cosmo must have associated the scent of burning peppers with the veeeep of the smoke alarm. She remembered the alarm after two months' time, and mimicked it perfectly.

Cosmo did not laugh, because she had not yet learned to laugh. But she must have enjoyed making me dash around the kitchen at top speed. She must have already developed a sense of humor.

This accomplishment of Cosmo's to create a practical joke, is truly remarkable. Imagine what went through her mind. Cosmo had smelled the roasting peppers, remembered the previous occasion and the amusement my unusually frenetic

activity had brought her. She associated the pungent scent of the peppers with the sound of the alarm, and then mimicked the alarm to prompt a repetition of my behavior. She knew that she was fooling me, because she shut her beak and stopped issuing the veeeep whenever I looked up.

That's significant mental activity for an animal who had hatched from a shell less than a year before.

It's significant physical activity, too. Cosmo made that very, very loud veeeep by whistling.

A parrot's anatomy is quite different from ours. Besides having feathers, a beak, and zygodactyl feet, a parrot also has a syrinx, an organ at the base of the trachea which we might call the bird's song box. A parrot, like most other birds, makes all her sounds by passing air in and out of the lungs through the syrinx. In other words, when Cosmo mimics a smoke alarm or a telephone ring or a woman laughing or a man talking, she does it by whistling.

Cosmo does an imitation of my voice good enough to deceive the PhD candidate in psychology who has been videotaping her. Cosmo uses a syrinx and I use a larynx to make the same sounds. Wow.

Not all birds have a syrinx. New World vultures make grunts and hisses, which sound little like bird calls, because they don't have a syrinx.

By the way, in Greek mythology Syrinx was a nymph whom the river gods transformed into hollow water reeds to save her from the amorous pursuits of the god Pan. Pan's breath caused the reeds to make the haunting sound of the panpipe.

Now Cosmo laughs riotously when she fools me. She knows what's funny. As I write, she is mimicking the ring of the phone—Rrring rrring rrring—to get me to come to her. So I leave my computer, go into the sunroom, pick up the phone, say "Hello," and then put it down. I look at her, and exclaim, "That's Cosmo!"

Cosmo laughs at the top of her little lungs. "That's Cosmo!" she repeats.

CHAPTER 22

Traces

THE SUNDAY AFTERNOON was dark and stormy. "It's raining," Cosmo observed.

No kidding. The rain was so heavy I considered building an ark. I figured that UPS could deliver the kit overnight in a huge box marked "easy to assemble."

Thunder cracked. "What's that?" Cosmo asked.

"That's thunder," I replied.

Cosmo then mimicked the beeps of a truck backing up, the ring of the phone, the bark of Kaylee and Mary, my laughter. She'll probably wait till the sun comes out to mimic the thunder.

I was lying on the sofa in Cosmo's room engrossed in a new mystery by Marcia Clark. I read mysteries, spy thrillers, and detective novels to educate myself in the ways of crime. Oops, I mean the ways of the law.

Anyway, today I learned about Edmond Locard (1877-1966), whom the French claimed as their Sherlock Holmes. Locard wrote, "Wherever he [the criminal] steps, whatever he touches, whatever he leaves, even unconsciously, will serve as a silent witness against him." Locard formulated the principle "Every contact leaves a trace" and set the agenda for today's forensic science.

Wow, I thought. Locard's Exchange Principle applies to everything that moves! We all leave traces of ourselves everywhere.

Locard was probably not concerned with everything that moves. He was concerned with human crooks and murderers. But I believe that many theories we humans develop for humans may apply to our fellow animals as well.

If Locard had gone to vet school instead of medical school, he might have considered the broader implications of his principle. But since animals don't seem to have as many criminals among themselves as we humans have among ourselves—I wonder why that is—he might not have found employment as a veterinary criminologist.

Now I'm thinking: Who better than a parrot bears unbiased witness to the traces of others upon her?

Cosmo conveys to me a multitude of environmental sounds to which I've been oblivious, such as the beeps of a truck backing up and the buzz of a leaf blower. And likewise she conveys to me the din of the woods: the calls of birds, the rat-a-tat-tat of woodpeckers, the screech of hawks, the hoot of owls, the chatter of squirrels, the songs of tree frogs and crickets. She gives me information I would not otherwise have when she mimics the sirens of the fire trucks and police cars that occasionally roar down the road nearby.

Cosmo differentiates the sounds of the world that are the sounds of nothing for people-oriented, self-indulgent, goal-focused, profit-driven, entertainment-motivated, computer-dependent, waste-producing, trash-littering, love-making, love-seeking, cell-phone-talking, text-messaging, web-surfing, email-sending, television-watching, working, playing, wining and dining, ever-so-busy humans. Just inconsequential background noise.

Those same sounds that Cosmo hears and repeats leave traces on me that I never notice. What would the absence of those sounds of nothing be like? Silence? I don't think I've ever known silence.

I leave traces of my existence on her and on all the other animals, vegetables, and minerals I bump up against in person or in writing, on the phone or on the web, in the woods or in my car, or in the effects of my consumption.

I like knowing that human, or non-human animal disappears completely into the past without leaving some evidence of having lived on Earth. Everybody influences history, not necessarily the history we humans tell ourselves of what humans do to other humans, but the total sequence of events over time. Everybody leaves tracks upon the planet.

If you'd like to determine the impact of your tracks upon the planet, that is, your ecological footprint, go to: http://my-footprint.org/en/visitor_information/.

My colleague Lioba Moshi told me that pet African grey parrots who have outlived their human are treasured in Tanzania for preserving the voice of the deceased for family and friends.

Cosmo speaks in my voice, at least most of the time. When I pass away, Cosmo will carry the traces of my existence into the future. She'll talk like me and laugh like me. She'll be my ghost. Hehe.

I usually say that parrots are like humans. Now I'll say that humans are like parrots, only not as talented at differentiating sounds. Like parrots we carry into the future the traces of our encounters.

If we are to make a happier world, our traces better be better than litter.

Chapter 23

Climate Change

THIS MORNING COSMO REFUSED to come with me to "Betty Jean's desk."

Instead, she climbed atop her roost cage to watch the wildlife activity on my deck railing. She called out to the four crows who were eating birdseed on the deck railing, "Caw caw!"

She spoke to a squirrel. "Squirrel, I love you."

She spoke to a cardinal. "Purdy purdy purdy."

She spoke to a Red-shouldered hawk. "Kee-aah kee-aah."

Then she barked for some reason known only to her. "Woo woo woo!"

Cosmo communicates in caws, chirps, and chatter with the birds, squirrels, and chipmunks who dine outside on our deck. She communicates in barks with my dogs, and in English with me and with company. She's friendly and she's multilingual.

Last summer when the temperature rose above a hundred degrees for a few days, I bought a concrete birdbath for the deck. In the early mornings and late afternoons, Cosmo and I watched a multitude of birds of different species drink with the squirrels from the same bowl. Some birds bathed. One crow took a piece of corn and dipped it into the water before eating it.

If I were not there with her to enjoy our outdoor menagerie, Cosmo would say quietly to herself, "That's birdy" or "That's squirrel."

What a peaceable kingdom. There was enough food and water for all. Everybody got along with everybody else.

I worry about how elevated summer temperatures affect

our non-human friends of the woods. If I had lost my air conditioning I would have had to take Cosmo to the Holiday Inn, for she might have died in temperatures above ninety degrees. I know that the Holiday Inn is pet-friendly, but I don't know how the hotel folks would have reacted to my bringing with me an overheated fawn or raccoon or skunk.

Anyway, animals need more than crisis care. They need for their home territory to stay the same with the same temperature ranges in winter and summer, the same vegetation, the same supply of water.

With rapid global climate change the present long-existing relationships of plants and animals in their home territory will not stay the same. Nearly all scientists consider our recent unusual heat an effect of global climate change.

The twelve-month period preceding the late June heat wave was the hottest on the United States mainland since record keeping began in 1895. Since 1990 our own region's average soil temperature has risen significantly, enough to prompt the Department of Agriculture, in February of 2012, to adjust our Hardiness Zone from 7B to 8A, the same as Albany, Georgia's. That means that farmers and gardeners here will be wise to grow plants and trees and fruits and vegetables that can survive a hotter, drier climate.

Our Georgia woods will change, as plants and trees that can't survive the hotter, drier climate will be supplanted by plants and trees that can. Our animal friends—mammals, birds, reptiles, insects, amphibians, etc.—may abandon the land that their ancestors have inhabited for decades, maybe centuries, maybe millennia, in order to find more favorable conditions. But they won't travel together, and they won't go to the same place. Some will die out. Our family will break up.

As our critters invade other critters' territories where the climate is cooler and wetter, either up north or at higher elevations, they will have to modify their diet, find different prey, munch on different vegetation, drink from different rivers and streams and lakes and ponds, and hang out with critters they've never met before. Their arrival will disrupt other families.

Here in Athens, we'll get new critters, such as armadillos. Perhaps eventually we'll get gila monsters.

And we'll be singing, "Where have all the cardinals gone?" The Audubon Society reports that cardinals are gradually moving northward in response to the rising temperatures.

If she lives to be fifty years old, Cosmo may be the only bird for miles around calling "purdy purdy purdy."

CHAPTER 24

Company

COSMO LOVES CHILDREN.

A few weeks ago, some young friends ages six, five, and three paid Cosmo a visit. They entered the front door, ran joyously to her cage in the dining room, and greeted her. "Hello, Cosmo!"

I had incarcerated Cosmo in anticipation of the children's arrival to keep her from accidentally flying off her perch in the thrill of it all. Cosmo poked her beak through the bars, looked the children over, and whistled. Chloe, Patrick, and Cormac giggled. Cosmo giggled. She whistled again. "Whee whew!"

When everybody had settled down in the living room, Cosmo told her jokes. "Rrring rrring rrring. Telephone for bird!" Then "Doggy has feathers!" "Cosmo gonna poop!" Each time Cosmo spoke, the children roared with laughter. So Cosmo roared with laughter.

Then Cosmo tried out various voices: "How are you?" in a man's voice. "Cosmo is a birdie!" in a voice I'd never heard before. "Cosmo wanna peanut!" in my voice.

If the children got quiet, Cosmo would pipe up with "Woo woo woo! That's doggy bark! Hahahahahaha!"

Cosmo was purposefully, and exuberantly, entertaining her young guests. She is less exuberant with guests my age. But guests my age are less exuberant than children.

I've thought about how both human and non-human animals recognize the young of other species. My female American Eskimo dogs have brought me baby birds and squirrels they've found and not harmed. They have also brought me adult chipmunks and voles they've killed.

In the first essay of her marvelous book Small Wonder, Barbara Kingsolver tells of a female bear in Iran rescuing and nursing a human toddler. Kingsolver believes that if a bear will save an infant of her enemy, we humans may hope that our international animosity will not extend to the young.

I have read many stories about adult animals of one species adopting or caring for infants of another. The practice is called "interspecies alloparenting." Alloparenting is parenting by individuals other than the actual parents. I guess I qualify as an interspecies alloparent.

On the web, we find videos and newspaper accounts like this: a crow protecting and feeding a kitten; a Dachshund providing a nipple to an orphaned piglet; a lioness adopting an Oryx calf; a gorilla cradling in her arms and taking to zoo-keepers a three-year-old human boy who had fallen into her enclosure at the Brookfield Zoo.

A friend told me that her horse, Lady, high-spirited and even rowdy with an adult in the saddle, walked slowly and cautiously when carrying a child.

Of course, many predators view the young of other species as easy prey. I'm sure my neighborhood hawks do not feel maternal when they spot a young mouse.

Most likely we recognize the young instinctively. In the 1970s, the famous Austrian zoologist Konrad Lorenz proposed that humans' preference for the faces of babies—both human and non-human—over the faces of adults was evolutionarily related to caregiving. Humans want to take care of babies, who tend to have a round face, protruding forehead, large eyes, and plump cheeks.

Walt Disney figured this out.

I find remarkable not just Cosmo's differentiation of children from adults but also the obvious pleasure she gets from entertaining them.

Cosmo acted as if Chloe, Patrick, and Cormac had come to visit her, not me, as if she, not I, were responsible for giving them a good time. She played the role of hostess.

At the end of their visit, Chloe, Patrick, and Cormac each held Cosmo briefly. With my assistance, Cosmo hopped up on their small outstretched arms and stayed very still. I think she knew she was a big bird for a little child to handle. After all, she weighs one pound and three-year-old Cormac weighs thirty-five.

Then the children and their parents donned their coats to leave. Cosmo told them "Good-bye," un-enthusiastically.

I have been accused of reading human emotions into Cosmo's behavior. I reply that I'm simply reading her emotions. Emotions do not belong to humans alone. Neither does kindness.

Like Kingsolver, I struggle to find in the occasional kindness of animals toward one another a model for fruitful human interaction.

CHAPTER 25

Bedtime

ONE SUMMER NIGHT long ago, when she was about two and a half years old, Cosmo expressed reluctance to be put to bed. I was finally able to lock her in her roost cage, say, "Good night, Cosmo, I love you," and close the door to her room.

As soon as I settled in my recliner in my bedroom, I heard from inside her darkened room "Cosmo wanna water!" I got up, opened her door, brought her fresh water, gave her a good-night kiss on her little warm beak, told her I loved her, and shut the door to her room.

I returned to my bedroom, sat down, picked up my book, and heard: "Cosmo wanna peanut!" I got up, went to the kitchen, took a handful of dry-roasted, unsalted peanuts, opened the door to her room, deposited the peanuts in her food dish, gave her a good-night kiss, told her I loved her, and shut the door to her room.

"Cosmo wanna cuddle!"

Oh, no!

"Cosmo wanna go up, okay?"

"Okay," I said.

Defeated, I let Cosmo out of her cage to have a few more minutes of quality time with me before beginning the bedtime ritual all over.

Parrots need ten-to-twelve hours of sleep a night. In the rain forests near the equator, African greys awaken at dawn and go to sleep at dusk. They do not stay up on their perches munching on palm nuts and chirping with each other late into the night, because they do not want to attract predators. Also, they can't see at night.

Parrots living in our homes need the same amount of sleep

as their wild kin, but sometimes they fail to get it. Whereas in the daytime, they need a large cage in the middle of family activity by a window for mental stimulation and entertainment, at night they need a roost cage in a darkened, quiet room for uninterrupted sleep. Without enough sleep, Greys become irritable, anxious, tired, and sometimes unhappy enough to pluck out their feathers.

That's why I try to put Cosmo to bed about nine o'clock, whether she wants to go or not. In June, when the days are long, she does not. In December she wants to go earlier. "Cosmo wanna go to bed," she'll say as soon as night falls.

Cosmo does take naps. Occasionally, in the afternoon, I spot her resting on one leg with the other drawn up under her belly and with her eyelids closed.

When birds go to sleep, they automatically lock their toes around their perch to keep from falling off. They often sleep on one foot only, preserving warmth by sheltering the other under their body.

Late one rainy, wintry night several hours after Cosmo had retired for the evening, I heard a ruckus and then a squawk in Cosmo's room. I leapt out of my chair, flung open the door, and found Cosmo standing on the bottom of her cage looking dazed. She'd flown off her perch. I picked her up and held her close. She was trembling.

She must have had a bad dream.

We know that humans are not the only animals who dream. Just as all of Earth's critters sleep, I assume that all of Earth's critters, at least the feathery, furry, and hairy ones, dream, often about each other and sometimes about humans. Everybody who has any mental life whatsoever must dream, and all animals have some sort of mental life. I love to imagine what hibernating bears dream about as well as and whales and skunks and hawks and possums.

I've been wondering what Cosmo dreams about. Does she dream about me, the love of her life, her caregiver, companion, cook, and driver? Does she dream about the dogs? Does she dream about the squirrels and the birds whom she watches during the day as they feed on the deck railing outside her window?

Does she dream about having company or going in a car?

Does she dream about her clutch mates and her parents, from whom she was separated in her first few months of life— she was sold to the pet store way too young to leave the nest? Her departure from her parents must have been traumatic to her.

Does she dream in English?

Does she have crazy dreams after eating too many peanuts?

Does she have nightmares about a hawk coming to get her, or the Dustbuster?

After we cuddled a bit, Cosmo said, "Como wanna go to bed."

CHAPTER 26

Instruction Manual

COSMO LOVES TO TEASE ME. And she's just a bird. Well, rather a special bird.

This morning Cosmo called me from high up on her perch in my bedroom. "Betty Jean, come here! Wanna kiss feathers?"

I did, of course. However, I do understand that the desire of humans to kiss feathers is not universal.

"Yes, Cosmo! I wanna kiss feathers! Come here," I answered. I stood on my tiptoes, but she was still more than twelve inches out of reach. She did not descend.

"Noooo," Cosmo said. "Cosmo don't wanna kiss feathers." And then she chuckled. "Hehehe."

I returned to the bathroom to finish putting on my make-up.

Immediately thereafter I heard, "Betty Jean, come here! Betty Jean wanna cuddle?"

I did. She didn't. She chuckled. "Hehehe."

Cosmo is a one-human bird. But then I'm a one-bird human. We are monogamous. I hope that our mutual affection does not hamper her ability to bond with members of another human family after my molecules have mingled with soil and air.

My friend Judy told me a story that caused me to ponder Cosmo's future. When Judy was a little girl, she loved a yellow-naped Amazon parrot named Polly. Polly lived across the street from Judy's country school house with Miss Lorena, Judy's grandmother. Miss Lorena had received Polly as a present from her brother in the early 1930s.

Miss Lorena and Polly were the star attraction of the neighborhood. Together they entertained Judy, her sister, and their countless little friends who preferred milk and cookies with Polly to reading and arithmetic with the schoolteacher. Polly talked,

Cosmo likes to cuddle.

laughed, whistled, and joyfully amused the adoring children.

When Miss Lorena died some fifteen years later, she bequeathed Polly to Judy, along with an instruction manual listing Polly's likes and dislikes, routine activities, and vocabulary words.

Judy, by now a young bride in a small apartment, did her best to make Polly happy, but she could not get her to talk. Polly must have been mourning the loss of Miss Lorena.

Judy and her husband read in the manual that Polly liked showers. They gave her one. As the water hit her, Polly cried out in Lorena's voice, "Polly's cold! Polly's cold!" Judy made the water warmer, and Polly fluffed her feathers in pleasure.

That shower was the beginning of a beautiful friendship. Polly immediately started talking, in Miss Lorena's voice. Polly traveled on road trips with Judy and her husband, welcomed the birth of their son, whom Polly called "Harold" when she first laid eyes on the infant even though Harold was not his name, and their daughter. Polly enjoyed the company of their cat and dog, and lived as an important member of their family for eighteen years. Polly used Miss Lorena's voice untill the day she died.

Although Polly must have been in her sixties when she died, Judy says Polly died way too young. Judy actually means way too soon. Judy misses her still.

In her voice Polly brought the memory of Miss Lorena into Judy's household. In her behavior Polly brought much more. Polly brought the sense of humor, desire for fun, and affection for others that she had acquired in her early years with Miss Lorena. That affection was reciprocated. Polly had a happy life.

That is what I hope for Cosmo.

Like Polly with Miss Lorena, Cosmo is attached to one person but acquainted with many. Fortunately, Cosmo knows that I'm not the only good human in the world, and although I suspect she'll miss me when I'm gone, she will probably love her future family as much as she loves me.

But I haven't told Cosmo's future family everything about Cosmo. I haven't told them that Cosmo expects to ride in the front seat when she goes "in a car," that Cosmo expects to be let out of her cage at sunrise, that Cosmo expects to share whatever I'm having for dinner, with the exception of wine and guaca- mole, and that Cosmo expects to be obeyed.

I'll put all that in the instruction manual as a little surprise for them.

CHAPTER 27

Grammatical Mistakes

THIS MORNING BEFORE BREAKFAST I approached Cosmo and asked, "Do you wanna go to kitchen?"

She bit me on my finger, not hard but deliberately, and replied, "That's Cosmo don't wanna go to kitchen."

I got her message.

A few moments later, Cosmo climbed down from her cage and followed me to the kitchen. "I'm here!" she announced.

"Hello, Cosmo!" I greeted her. I don't hold a grudge.

"Cosmo wanna go up," she said.

Erin Colbert-White, who had gotten her PhD in comparative psychology with a dissertation on Cosmo's speech, once asked me, "Why does Cosmo start so many sentences with 'that's?"

What do you expect? I thought to myself. What's grammar to a bird? But I answered her question.

"Cosmo probably started attaching 'That's' to a sentence when I first held her up to a mirror and said, 'That's Cosmo!'"

Now Cosmo looks at her reflection and says, "That's Cosmo is whatta bird." She hears Mary bark and says, "That's Mary bark," or "that's doggy bark—woo woo woo."

Cosmo's grammatical mistakes are legion:

> "Cosmo are here!"
> "Where wanna gonna go?"
> "Cosmo wanna we're gonna go in a car."
> "Betty Jean wanna hafta go to work?"
> "Cosmo go wanna be a good bird."
> "Cosmo don't be a good bird."
> "Cosmo wanna go be kiss."
> "Doggy has bark."
> "Time for let's go to kitchen Cosmo."

"Where's Cosmo are?"
"We're gonna have . . . time to go to work!"
"Cosmo wanna be go to kitchen.
"Wanna go to Betty Jean kiss? Smooch! Thank you!"
"Cosmo wanna be go up!"

Her mistakes reveal that she understands what the words mean. She's not copying me. I've never said "Betty Jean wanna hafta go to work," but I've said "Betty Jean wanna go in a car" and "I hafta go to work." What I find amazing is that Cosmo uses words in different contexts to say what she wants. And she makes sentences.

I didn't teach Cosmo to talk. Cosmo learned to talk from me. There's a difference. Since I spoke to her from the moment she came into my home at the age of six months, Cosmo learned that everything—things, actions, individuals—has a name. She's adapted to her world by using my words. That's how she exercises control over her environment.

We all want to exercise control over our environment, with either speech or behavior. Cosmo is capable of using speech to do it because she has the intellectual equipment to understand us and the physical equipment—a syrinx, which is a bird's vocal organ—to speak like us. Dogs have the intellectual equipment but not the physical equipment.

Still, for Cosmo, English is a foreign language. She's doing her best to speak it.

Some linguists would not approve of my calling Cosmo's speech "language." They say that language is characterized by grammar and that only humans use language. To me, they're engaging in a debate over the definition of language. I'll grant that humans use grammar better than anybody else. We can write novels, poems, and columns in the *Athens Banner-Herald.* Cosmo can't.

But why dwell on our grammatical superiority? I don't want to judge anybody's ability to communicate meaningfully on the basis of grammar. I'm just happy that the linguistic research with parrots and great apes has stimulated our investigation into animal communication in general.

New technology has helped too. Scientists employing digital recording devices have discovered that all kinds of birds and mammals communicate meaningfully with each other. Some of them, including wild parrots, crows, numerous other birds as well as dolphins and whales even have regional accents.

Some birds are bilingual, capable of using both their local song to communicate with their neighbors and a second dialect to communicate with migrating birds. See the Fisher Science Education website on "Animals with Accents."

And would you believe it? A few birds may be grammatical after all. Japanese researchers have detected implicit grammatical rules in bird songs. As reported in the journal New Scientist on June 26, 2011, Kentaro Abe of Kyoto University has found that Bengal Finches recognize in their songs the difference between appropriate and inappropriate syntax.

My take-home lesson is that everybody's talking. We grammatical humans just didn't know it until recently. We had not listened.

Now we know that trillions of critters are telling each other what's going on. The hills, valleys, woods, plains, mountains, deserts, rivers, and seas are alive with the sound of chatter.

Chapter 28

Feeding the Birds

ONE DAY COSMO CALLED TO ME from atop her roost cage:
"Look, birdies!" Wow. There must have been forty goldfinches
plus a woodpecker and a couple of cardinals eating the food
I'd put out on the deck railing.

To attract the birds to Cosmo's restaurant, I serve up a
good cocktail: thistle, safflower seed, sunflower seed, peanuts,
corn, and a mysterious commercial concoction advertised for
"colorful birds." I also keep water in a bird bath available for
them throughout the year.

Birds can get anything they want at Cosmo's restaurant. So
can squirrels.

I'm always amazed that Cosmo, a sixteen-ounce African
grey parrot, recognizes little finches, big crows, doves, woodpeckers, cardinals, and blue jays all as birdies, like herself.

And Cosmo knows what she looks like. She says, gazing at
her reflection in the mirror, "Cosmo is a birdie!"

I watched a PBS show on crows with Cosmo perched on
the back of my chair. Cosmo cried, "Caw caw" every time she
spotted a crow on the screen. That was often. I felt like I was
watching the program in stereo.

More than fifty-five million of us Americans feed wild
birds, and together we spend more than three billion dollars
on bird food and more than eight hundred million dollars on
bird-feeding accessories. Some of my friends who like birds
better than squirrels seem to be on a lifelong quest for a squir-
rel-proof bird feeder. I like birds and squirrels equally. I want
them all to feel at home at Cosmo's restaurant.

Some critics argue out that feeding the birds in our back
yard changes the relationships of species to each other in the

wild. It increases disproportionately the populations of birds who like thistle, safflower seed, sunflower seed, peanuts, corn, and the mysterious commercial concoction advertised for colorful birds.

Others tell us that feeding the birds spreads avian diseases by bringing the birds into unnaturally close proximity to each other, that it makes birds dependent on humans, that it changes their normal diet, that it disrupts their natural behavior.

All this may be true but, as my mentor ecologist Eugene Odum used to say, "Let's see what else may be true."

Feeding the birds in our back yard enables us to view our feathered inhabitants of Earth up close and personal. It expands our knowledge of different species. It gets us interested in the lives of animals unlike ourselves. It makes us wonder where the crows and finches and cardinals and woodpeckers go when they're not dining at Cosmo's restaurant.

In the long run, feeding wild birds may make us humans more protective of our natural environment. It raises our sensitivity to the potentially harmful impact of human activity on our planet's wildlife. That's good for the whole wide world.

By the way, we humans have shared our bounty with our wild avian friends for centuries. In the fifteenth century, the Ottoman Turks constructed on the sides of their architecturally magnificent buildings equally ornate birdhouses with multiple compartments for finches, sparrows, and swallows.

In the sixteenth century, the Dutch made clay birdhouses, originally to trap birds and secure their eggs but later to protect the birds against inclement weather.

In the eighteenth century, English and German immigrants learned from Native Americans to make birdhouses out of birch bark with a platform as a feeder.

Does feeding the birds incline us to be kinder, gentler humans? I'd say yes.

I feed the wild birds because Cosmo can't. Nobody will visit her if she doesn't provide refreshments. And she loves their company. So do I.

Cosmo got her education in bird calls from her restaurant. She can mimic the voice of everybody who comes here.

But Cosmo is not mimicking bird calls this morning. While the birds and squirrels eat my birdseed cocktail, Cosmo is whistling the first four lines of Leonard Cohen's 1967 song "Hey, That's No Way to Say Good-bye" over and over.

I should probably teach her to whistle the Sherman Brothers' 1964 song "Feed the Birds," which Julie Andrews sang in the movie *Mary Poppins*.

Cosmo loves music "What's that?

Chapter 29

Music

"WHERE ARE YOU? There you are!" Cosmo crossed the hall, looked my way, commented, and then entered her room. Cosmo, my African grey parrot, goes wherever she likes in the house, but she wants to know my whereabouts at all times.

Cosmo called to me, "Betty Jean wanna whistle?" and commenced a medley of our favorite tunes expecting a duet. I complied.

When I whistle a tune unfamiliar to her, Cosmo listens intently and tries to reproduce it. She's a quick learner. She's learned, a bit imperfectly, I confess, parts of "Zippidy-Doo-Dah," "Heigh-Ho," "Bridge on the River Quai," "Yankee Doodle," "Wooden Heart," and the Meow Mix song. But these days she almost never whistles any one tune in its entirety.

Cosmo treats music the way she treats language. To communicate with me in English she puts together words to make sentences. Correct sentences, such as "Do you wanna go to Betty Jean's desk?" and incorrect but equally meaningful ones, such as "Here are you?" and "Cosmo wanna gonna go in a car" and "That's Cosmo is a good birdie."

We may chuckle at Cosmo's efforts, but that's how humans talk. We put together in new ways words we already know to convey thoughts we consider original.

When Cosmo whistles she puts together fragments of melodies she already knows in new combinations, plus a few bird songs, to make compositions she's proud of. She'll whistle exuberantly for minutes on end, pausing only to congratulate herself. "Wow! What a bird!"

Cosmo likes my music too, especially vocal music, to which she whistles original accompaniments. She always asks to dance when I play Mexican mariachi music on high volume.

According to some recent research, cats and monkeys like music, but not the kind humans like. Professor Charles Snowdon of the University of Wisconsin says that the music an individual can enjoy emotionally is related to his species's vocal range and heart rate. Not everybody has the same heart rate.

Snowdon had National Symphony cellist David Teie composed a couple of songs for Tamarin monkeys, who have a heartbeat twice as fast as the human heartbeat and a vocal range three octaves higher than the human vocal range. Teie played the songs on his cello and then electronically boosted them to monkey-voice pitch. Teie's fast song—let's call it monkey rock—excited the Tamarins. The slow music calmed them down and made them sociable, sort of lovey-dovey. Both were way too shrill and high tempo for humans to enjoy. Darn. Tamarins and humans would not be good dance partners, anyway. Tamarins are the size of squirrels.

Even though Snowdon and Teie are now making feline-specific music, Snowdon says that neither cats nor monkeys nor any other animals will love music the way we humans do. He says that only humans have relative pitch, and that only humans recognize the relationships between the notes with a change of key.

I beg to differ. I want Professor Snowdon to meet Cosmo, who can start "Meow-Mix" just about anywhere on the scale and produce an identifiable rendition of the ditty. I suspect that Cosmo likes my music because her vocal range is similar to mine, even though her heart rate is faster. A human's heart rate varies between fifty and eight-four beats per minute, depending on the individual's age and health. University of Georgia researcher Branson Ritchie reports that the African grey parrot's heart rate varies between three hundred forty and six hundred beats per minute.

The *Oxford English Dictionary* defines music as "The art or science of combining vocal or instrumental sounds with a view to beauty or coherence of form and expression of emotion."

I don't know whether Cosmo is making "music" when she whistles, since her compositions seem pretty formless, but she's certainly expressing joy. And she certainly feels joy in the music of mine she hears.

I like to imagine that the furry and feathery animals in our world, whose hearts beat in different tempos, who vocalize and hear in different ranges, can all be moved emotionally by the music of the planet that is theirs.

Chapter 30

Dinnertime

COSMO LOVES TO HAVE company, human company. When she sees me set the dining room table, she says with great delight, "We're gonna have company!" When the guests arrive, she says, "We've got company!"

The only disadvantage Cosmo sees to having company is that I occasionally put her back into her dining room cage to keep her from nipping an ankle or a toe. There she can hear us in the living room but not see us.

Cosmo begs to be let out. Our conversation like this:

> Cosmo: "Cosmo wanna go up. Please?"
> Betty Jean: "No. Cosmo stay in cage. Okay?"
> Cosmo: "Cosmo be a good bird."
> Betty Jean: "Cosmo stay in cage. We've got company."
> Cosmo: "Cosmo don't bite. Okay?"
> Betty Jean: "Cosmo stay in cage."
> Cosmo: "Cosmo don't poop on floor. Cosmo go up, okay?"
> Betty Jean: "Okay."

If I don't accede to her pleas, Cosmo will try to participate in our conversation. She tells her jokes: "Telephone for Cosmo!" and "Mary has feathers!" And then she laughs boisterously. If she hears the guests laugh, she laughs some more. If she knows that the guests are eating cashews, she calls out, "Cosmo wanna peanut!"

Yet when humans sit down to eat, Cosmo preens quietly on the perch atop her cage, contented simply to be with us.

On occasion at dinner—but only with my most relaxed, congenial, indulgent, laidback, lenient, liberal, open-minded, good-natured, easy-going, Cosmo-loving friends—Cosmo has hopped on the table to forage from everybody's plate. She especially appreciates watermelon and mango. She also likes cake and she loved the cake with her image copied onto the frosting that I got her for her hatchday party. I noticed that she was the last to take a bite.

Even though Cosmo lives in an environment foreign to her species, in a house with two dogs and a human, I try to figure out what she would be naturally inclined to do. It's much easier to influence her cultural behavior if I'm building on her instinctual behavior.

For example, wild African grey parrots spend day and night with their flock. In the wild, individual parrots are almost never isolated from their flock, with whom they feel safe from predators. In accepting my dogs and me as her flock, Cosmo has already deviated from her instinctual need to be with other greys. In order to keep her happy, we must act as her flock, as best we featherless folk can.

Cosmo's wild African relatives eat together. Therefore, Cosmo joins me at mealtimes. She eats whenever I eat, and sometimes whatever I eat, with the exception of avocado, chocolate, wine, and coffee, which are toxic to parrots. She likes ZuPreem FruitBlend Premium parrot food "with 21 vitamins and minerals in every bite," as well as bananas, oranges, raw cashews, hard-boiled eggs, sugar peas, Rock Cornish game hens, saffron and prawn pasta, and just about anything else that is served.

Cosmo goes with me wherever I go in the house. If for some reason I temporarily put her in her cage, she will call out to me as loudly as she needs to, "I'm here!" That's natural. She's telling me where she is and reminding me that we should not be separated.

Yesterday I came home late from a dinner to find the dogs impatient for their bedtime snack. First I let Cosmo out of her cage in my bedroom, where she likes to stay with the dogs when I am gone for the evening, and then I followed Kaylee

Dinner time. Cosmo got company.

and Mary to the kitchen.

As I was cutting little chunks of summer sausage for their treat, I heard Cosmo hurrying down the dark hallway to join us. "Here I am," she announced as she entered the kitchen. She looked up expectantly. I gave her a chunk too.

Cosmo has learned the culture of my household. When company has stayed long enough, in her opinion, she says sweetly, from her perch on her dining room cage, "Time to go to bed!" She repeats it as often as necessary.

And when the guests go down the hall to the front door, Cosmo follows, with Kaylee on one side of her and Mary on the other, and says, "Good-bye."

CHAPTER 31

Owls and Hawks

LATE ONE SPRING NIGHT, I heard the familiar call of the barred owl: "Who cooks for you, who cooks for you all?"

So the next morning I pulled up a YouTube video of a barred owl to make sure I had identified the bird correctly. I turned the sound up high. From her room Cosmo heard the owl's call, waddled down the hall into my study, climbed atop her cage, turned to the computer screen with the video of the owl, and informed me, "That's a birdie!"

Until recently I thought that the barred owl was a "bard" owl, a singing poet of the avian world. That still makes sense to me.

As Cosmo and I studied the computer screen together, I said to myself: How lovely! Cosmo and I are having similar thoughts. We both like owls.

But actually, a two-pound owl would eat a one-pound parrot if it could. If Cosmo saw or heard a barred owl in the woods, she would avoid him.

Apparently, Cosmo feels safe with me inside my house.

How did Cosmo know that the owl on the screen was a bird but not a threat to her? Cosmo would know a predator in the wild.

An owl is a predator. Predator animals, like cougars and humans, have eyes close together in front of their head, in order to focus clearly on prey. An owl is an obvious predator.

Cosmo is prey. Prey animals, like rabbits and gazelles, have eyes far apart with almost 360-degree vision to see predators coming after them. Cosmo is obvious prey.

Did Cosmo recognize the call of the owl coming out of my

computer as the call of a bird?

Or did she recognize the image of the barred owl as the image of a bird? If so, what clue did the owl give to inform Cosmo that he was a bird and not a possum? Cosmo had never seen an owl, not ever.

I decided to test Cosmo. My neighbors had alerted me to the red-tailed hawks live cam on the Cornell Lab of Ornithology website. A red-tailed hawk is a raptor, like the owl. A raptor seizes his prey with his talons.

I opened the website. That day the mother hawk was feeding the remains of a freshly seized squirrel to her three chicks. Either she or her husband, the father hawk, had brought it back to the nest. Red-tailed hawks mate for life and share parental responsibilities.

When the image of the mother hawk filled my computer screen, Cosmo, from atop the cage behind me, immediately said, "That's a birdie." Neither the mother hawk nor her offspring had made a sound. She watched the screen intently and repeated several times, "That's a birdie!"

I figured that Cosmo had come to that conclusion from seeing the video of the hawks.

For me, the hawks were not easy to see, since the adults were brown and the nest was brown, and the little chicks, fuzzy balls of white feathers, had only tiny beaks to show they were birdies. And Cosmo was at least five feet away from the computer screen.

I had to remind myself that Cosmo's vision is far sharper than mine, since she sees into the ultraviolet ranges of light, and her hearing is far more acute then mine. She sees and hears things that I do not.

After a while I pulled myself away from the fascinating maternal activity of the hawk and followed Cosmo back into her room. The website remained up. Ten minutes later the little chicks chirped. Cosmo listened and announced, "That's a birdie."

The next morning Cosmo and I pulled up the hawk website again and expanded the image to fill the screen. The mother hawk was feeding her chicks bits of a fresh chipmunk. I could see the chipmunk's tail. Cosmo repeated again and again with great excitement, "That's a birdie!"

Thank goodness she did not notice the chipmunk.

I looked carefully at the hawks' nest. There was almost enough fur from adorable recently deceased little critters to make a blanket for a mouse.

By the way, since these hawks use the same nest year after year, which they freshen up in late winter, the nest accumulates the little bones of squirrels, mice, rabbits, chipmunks, and other small animals. An archeologist's dream.

While monitoring the hawks, I was also trying to write a newspaper column. But I felt guilty every time I switched from Cosmo's reality television show to my document. I bet Cosmo was chagrined that I controlled the remote.

Chapter 32

Independence

"COSMO WANNA GO UP! Cosmo don't bite, okay? Cosmo don't poop on floor, okay? Cosmo go up! Please? Cosmo wanna be a good bird."

Cosmo is, in her words, "back in cage." She wants out. She'll promise anything to get me to open her cage door.

I open the door, and she pops out. Cosmo is a "good bird" while she perches on top of her cage. She is "good" for about two minutes. Then she climbs off the cage and heads for the telephone cord, the third one I've installed in the last six weeks.

I grab her. She bites me, not hard but deliberately.

Then she looks up and says, "That hurt? Cosmo bad bird. Go back in cage."

I'm not sure that Cosmo ever wants to be a good bird.

She's not bothered a bit when I scold her, when I tell her she's a "bad bird."

To Cosmo, being a good bird means pleasing me. It means being subordinate to me, obeying my wishes, following my rules. It means not being independent. It means not following her natural inclinations. Why should she want to be a good bird?

Subordination to a human is unnatural for Cosmo, or for any animal with the wild still in her. Independence is natural.

Here's a big difference between wild animals and domesticated animals, between birds and dogs, for instance. Parrots are still wild animals, though tamable as individuals. Dogs are domesticated animals, produced by artificial selection. Subordination to humans is natural for dogs, or rather for most dogs.

Dogs have co-habited with humans for tens of thousands of years. Over this time, we have selectively bred them to live with us, to obey us, to follow our rules, to please us. We've bred border collies to herd our sheep and Jack Russell terriers to help us hunt. Doberman Pinschers guard us and Papillons to sit on our laps. We praise them for doing the job we bred them to do naturally, and for obeying us.

If I say "Good dog!" to Mary, an American Eskimo dog whose talent I've yet to discover, she wags her tail. She delights in my approval. If I say "Bad dog!" she hides under the bed. She's ashamed.

We tend to call individuals "good" or "bad" according to how obedient they are to our rules. We say they're "good" if they do what we ask of them and "bad" if they don't. We expect them to try to be good.

But some don't care. Can you imagine telling a squirrel "Bad squirrel" and motivating him to get off a bird feeder? Or telling a hawk "Bad hawk" and shaming her into releasing the cute little chipmunk she was planning to take to her nestlings for dinner? Or telling a grizzly "Bad bear!" and embarrassing him into releasing you?

Unless we're shouting at the top of our lungs, we're unlikely to influence these wild animals by a reprimand. They are doing what comes naturally to them. Why would they limit their freedom to please humans?

Why would Cosmo?

I doubt that pleasing a foreign power comes naturally to anybody, other than our dearly beloved dogs.

I've mentioned before how often Cosmo says "No" to my requests, suggestions, and invitations. In fact, she'll ask "Betty Jean wanna kiss?" and when I'm just about to put my lips to her beak, she'll say "No," back away, and laugh. She decides when to kiss, not I, although she sometimes chooses to grant my request for a kiss. After all, I'm her significant other, her friend, her caregiver. We're bonded.

Nonetheless, Cosmo is often a "good bird." She cuddles with me, talks with me, calls to me, whistles duets with me. She does all that not because I ask her but because she wants to. And I do almost all she asks of me because I want to.

Cosmo must see an advantage for herself in our togetherness. That is probably the only reason she sometimes obeys.

Cosmo has very admirably made a fine life for herself confined in my house with my dogs and me. She is happy. She has figured out how to have fun in an environment that her wild grandparents in Africa could not have imagined and would not have survived.

As her human, I control her time in cage, but I don't control her spirit.

PART II

Cosmo and Her Fellow Residents of Earth

Photo by Betty Jean Craige

Chapter 33

Time

"TIME FOR SHOWER for Cosmo in Cosmo room," Cosmo said one morning after I'd gotten out of my shower.

With that long sentence, Cosmo pointed out that it was her turn to be sprayed with water.

Cosmo knows when it's time for my shower, for her shower, for us to go to kitchen, and for her to go to bed. On occasion she has said, ungrammatically but appropriately, "Time for Betty Jean go to work."

Anybody living with a dog or a cat will not be surprised that Cosmo knows the household schedule. Cosmo has a Betty Jean clock, which guides most of her daily activities.

Cosmo also has an African grey clock, which guides the rest: waking and sleeping, vocalizing and keeping silent, flying and feeding on the ground.

Oops. She doesn't fly because her flight feathers are clipped. and she eats from a dish.

Cosmo does her best to adapt to her Betty Jean world, because that's where the fun is. Of course, she knows no other world.

Occasionally, Cosmo has a conflict. Her African grey clock tells her to go to sleep, while her Betty Jean clock tells her to stay up. But she handles the conflict like a mature adult. For example, when guests stay at the dinner table past her bedtime, Cosmo will declare "Time to go to bed," alerting the guests to the lateness of the evening.

Or she starts saying softly, "Good-bye."

I have to remind myself of the enormity of Cosmo's adaptation to my world. She has developed not only speech skills but also self-reliance and independence as an individual that her African kin would not develop.

In Africa, Cosmo's wild relatives do not exhibit individuality. Individualism is not one of their values. African greys in the rain forest are completely dependent on their flock mates for safety. And their flock mates are all African greys. Picture five hundred African greys, all looking just like Cosmo, flying together and landing together. And even though we know they're among the smartest birds on Earth, we'd look at them acting in unison and say, "That's groupthink!"

Actually, it's not groupthink. Each bird in the flock is simply monitoring very closely the actions of the individual birds next to him. That is, a bird watches the bird to his left, the bird to his right, the bird above, and the bird below, and he moves in sync with them. This ability is critical to everybody's survival. Here's where peer pressure is beneficial.

By forming a huge gray mass when they forage on the ground or when they fly, the grey parrots are safe from hawks, who cannot distinguish individual birds in the flock to seize as prey. The Greys fly, feed, and sleep together.

Cosmo has accomplished much intellectually to be a "good bird" in her Betty Jean world. Her African grey instinctual urges tell her not to hang out with animals, including other birds, who do not resemble her. Her Betty Jean social obligations compel her to get along with two dogs and a human who has lots of human company.

Her African grey instinctual urges tell her to go to bed when darkness comes. Her Betty Jean social obligations compel her to stay up as long as there's activity to enjoy.

However, her African Grey instinctual urges also tell her to stay with others, and that coincides with her Betty Jean social obligations.

Last night I had an impromptu party with neighbors that started at ten thirty, when Cosmo was ready to go to sleep. But she got excited when "we got company," and she wanted to stay up with us.

At one point, however, when we had stopped paying attention to her, she left us to go into her room. I figured she was going to sleep.

But Cosmo did not go to sleep. Instead, she whistled at the top of her lungs a medley of tunes she'd learned and tunes she'd composed, complete with glorious trills and warbles. After maybe a minute of this melody, Cosmo paused. The humans shouted praise to her. After a moment of silence Cosmo continued with a new composition, equally complex and delightful, for another minute. Again she paused. The humans called out, "Good whistle, Cosmo! Wow! Whatta bird!" We got an encore.

I think Cosmo knew she was making beautiful music. At least she knew we liked it. Would she create her own unique melodies to entertain avian flock mates? I doubt it.

Chapter 34

Animal Minds

THIS MORNING I AWOKE to the piercing siren of a police car.

Suddenly the siren stopped. And Cosmo called out from her room, "Come here! Cosmo wanna go up! Cosmo wanna poop!"

Whew! For a moment I thought the police had come to get me. I'd rather have awakened to "Heigh–Ho."

Cosmo mimics just about everything she hears. The police must have recently roared down my street.

Cosmo is not just smart. She's witty. She enjoys startling me, and she is well aware that the police siren will get my attention, like the smoke alarm. She's right.

Now that we know that parrots are smart, we're passing laws to protect them. We're passing laws to protect the great apes for the same reason, we know they're smart.

The cover story of the March 2008 *National Geographic*, titled "Inside Animal Minds," featured a few individuals who were truly brainy. There was Betsy, a border collie from Austria, who showed knowledge of three hundred forty words. There was Kanzi, a bonobo from the Iowa Primate Learning Sanctuary, who communicated through more than three hundred sixty keyboard symbols, understood thousands of spoken words, and formed sentences. There was Betty, a wild-caught New Caledonian crow residing at Oxford University in England, who bent a wire into a hook to retrieve a piece of meat from a glass tube.

And there was JB, a beautiful red giant Pacific octopus from the National Aquarium in Baltimore, who recognized the Aquarium staff as individuals, played with them, and amused himself by shooting water at targets.

Public attention to animal intelligence has pricked our social conscience. It has fundamentally altered our attitude toward animals whose lives we humans control—pets, livestock, zoo animals, and research animals—as well as their wild kinfolk whose lives we think we don't control. We feel guilty that we've abused animals who have thoughts and feelings like ours, and we're passing laws to protect them. Hooray.

But I'd hate to use intelligence, by which we usually mean resemblance to our smart selves, as a criterion for deciding whom we save. We don't do that for members of our own species.

Since octopuses, crows, apes, and everybody else on Earth are parts of a system, an ecosystem, I think we should focus on preserving the whole system rather than particular components. If we just protect smart animals we may accidentally ignore the earthworm, for example, whose intelligence is not obvious but whose job in nature may be more important to the planet's stability than the obviously intelligent bonobo's.

As the bumper sticker says, "Save the planet." The real meaning is: "Save the planet in its present condition hospitable to humans." Or "Save the planet for humans."

Why not save the planet for everybody?

The best way to help everybody is to clean up Earth. We've found out that when we toss garbage onto our land, into our rivers and seas, and into our air, we unintentionally recycle it back through the bodies of octopuses, crows, apes, dogs, parrots, frogs, fish, and cows, and ourselves. When we flush our medicines down the toilet we pass them onto folks without prescriptions. I won't go into details about how pharmaceutical pollution happens.

I don't want any of us to drink water polluted by other folks' used pharmaceuticals. We might get strange. Or less brainy. Or less sexy.

Think about how pharmaceutical waste alone is affecting Earth's inhabitants. In pharmaceutically polluted waters researchers have discovered effeminate male fish with lower

117

sperm counts and decreased interest in sexual activity as well as male smallmouth bass with premature egg cells in their testes. And shrimp behaving weirdly, as if intoxicated, from exposure to the antidepressant Prozac.

The animals in streams and oceans who weren't given prescriptions for oral contraceptives, antidepressants, and tranquilizers are having to take the same drugs some of us take because humans have accidentally medicated Earth.

I try to keep Cosmo safe. I don't leave ibuprofen on the bathroom counter. I don't use Teflon pans, which emit toxic fumes when overheated. Or scented candles. Or air freshener. I don't want Cosmo to get less brainy.

I don't want anybody to get less brainy, not you, not me, not Cosmo, Mary, or Kaylee, not octopuses, crows, apes, or dogs, not voles or frogs or fish, not the cattle we raise to eat, not even the possums contemplating a trip to the other side of the road.

Imagine an unmedicated Earth in which individuals of all species flourish, use whatever brains they have, do the job that nature has assigned them, and pursue life, liberty, and happiness as best they can. Imagine. It's easy if you try.

Chapter 35

Voices

Last night driving home in the dark after having dinner with friends, Cosmo said to me, "Cosmo go in a car." We were stopped at an intersection. I put my fingers into her cage, and Cosmo seized them with her toes in an embrace.

She said, "I love you."

I said to her, "I love you."

For Cosmo, as a television commercial says, the moment had turned romantic.

Today, Cosmo is perched atop her cage behind me whistling and making kissing sounds. She just said, "I love you," but I was concentrating on this column and did not respond. So she repeated, this time loudly and insistently, "I love you!"

That got my attention. I replied, in my sweetest tone, "I love you, Cosmo." I won't make that mistake again. I want her to know that when she speaks to me, I speak to her. When she calls to me, I call back.

I am Cosmo's significant other, or from her perspective— her mate. African grey parrots mate for life.

So do most parrots, as well as cardinals and crows. According to Mother Nature Network, we can add to the list of sexually faithful spouses bald eagles, swans, black vultures, albatrosses, and turtle doves, as well as wolves, gibbons, prairie voles, and French angelfish.

I have wondered how the birds choose and recognize their mates.

Cosmo didn't have a great choice for a mate in my household it was either a dog or me. She chose me.

But in the wild, parrots prefer to pair up with individuals of their own kind. So how would a female African grey recognize the love of her life? According to some researchers, most birds have a poor sense of smell, and African greys are no exception. So an African grey would not recognize her mate by smell.

Would she recognize her mate by sight? Even with their outstanding vision, far superior to our human vision, parrots might have difficulty spotting their mate in a flock of a thousand greys. Greys look a lot alike to us humans, and they might look somewhat alike to other greys.

Moreover, African Grey males and females do not differ in appearance from each other externally. Like most parrots— with the exception of the eclectus parrot, where the females are red and purple and the males are green—greys are monomorphic.

But we're not birds, and birds must be able to tell males and females apart.

What matters is that greys don't sound alike to each other, nor do birds of any other species sound alike to each other. According to James Northern of the Moore Laboratory of Zoology at Occidental College, every bird has a unique voice. Northern writes,

> Birds recognize each other by their voices or calls. They can identify mates, parents or offspring by voice, much as a blind person might do. During courtship and pair formation, birds learn to recognize their mate by 'voice' characteristics, and not by visual appearance.

Wow.

Every one of the hawks soaring above the trees, every one of the crows flying among the trees, every one of the woodpeckers drilling into the trees, and every one of the finches sharing birdseed with the squirrels on my deck has his or her own unique voice which at least his or her mate recognizes.

We should not be surprised. Humans all have unique voices too, which we recognize whether or not we are looking at each other. So do our pet dogs, cats, and horses. We recognize their unique barks, meows, and neighs. One woman told me recently that two hours after giving birth she recognized her baby's cry in the hospital nursery down the hall from her room.

In the wild, African grey parrots learn a variety of calls: contact calls—such as "I'm here! Where are you?"—alarm calls, food-begging calls, and calls of aggression. Even in flocks as large as eight-hundred birds, the individuals can find their parents, their siblings, and their mates by the sound of their voices.

Humans get to hear—the wondrous symphony of birds' calls to each other mainly at dawn when the birds awaken and take flight, and at dusk when the birds return to their roost.

Cosmo mimics their calls perfectly: the oo-wah-hoo-oo-oo courtship call of the male mourning dove; the purdy purdy purdy of the cardinal; the jaay jaay of the blue jay; the raucous caw caw of the crows; the soft haunting cry of the chuck will's widow.

Mimicking the calls she hears is part of Cosmo's early morning ritual. I awaken to the lovely sounds of a thousand birds, but I'm never quite sure which calls emanate from the woods and which ones emanate from Cosmo's room across the hall. That is, not until I hear Cosmo interrupt the symphony with a shrill "I'm here! Where are you?"

I answer, "I'm here! I'm coming."

Chapter 36

A Job

Oʜ, ɴo! Cosmo got into the dogs' cookie jar!

I'd left Cosmo on her dining-room cage to go get my mail. When I returned I discovered that she'd abandoned her perch, walked to the other end of the kitchen, opened a cabinet door, climbed onto the shelves and then onto the counter, made her way to the plastic cookie jar, and removed its plastic lid. She was poised to grab a cookie when I rescued her. Actually I rescued the cookies.

I can't get mad at her. Cosmo is simply exploring her territory. I don't want her to know that everything she likes belongs not to her but to me: the cookies, the pots and pans, the towels, the dental floss, the lipsticks, the pens, the telephone cord, the baseboards, and in fact, everything in the house and the house itself.

I'm constantly removing something from her beak, constantly telling her, "No, Cosmo!" Sometimes, "Please, Cosmo, be a good bird!" Occasionally, "Cosmo is bad bird. Cosmo go back in cage."

I am like the five-year-old host who declares "That's mine" whenever the four-year-old guest touches anything.

Cosmo knows nothing about ownership. What she knows is that my house is her home, that my dogs are her companions, that I am her favorite. We're her flock, imperfect as we are, having no feathers.

Ownership—that is, ownership of something beyond one's immediate physical grasp—is a human concept. Legally I own the lot on which my house sits, but I share it with woodpeckers, hawks, and countless other birds, as well as squirrels, chipmunks, raccoons, possums, snails, and insects. Deer visit.

So do coyotes. They don't know they're trespassing on my land.

One morning while I was working in my study I heard a sudden knocking on the wall.

Oh, no, I thought. My house is being destroyed by woodpeckers. How can I get rid of them?

I googled woodpeckers. I learned that woodpeckers eat insects in the tree bark. They keep the trees healthy if the insects haven't already done fatal damage. Thank you, Woody!

I googled squirrels. I found that squirrels transport nuts and seeds from one place to another. They don't know that that's their job in the ecosystem, but they do it anyway. After they bury an acorn in the fall to eat in the winter, they sometimes forget where they've put it. The acorn sprouts in the spring and grows into an oak tree. Squirrels plant trees!

Coyotes keep the squirrel population under control. Thanks, Wile E.

What do possums do? According to the National Opossum Society, possums are nature's sanitation workers. They eat the carcasses of their woodland neighbors, and they keep the snail population under control. Three cheers for possums.

How about humans? I guess we humans keep the deer population under control. And then we push up daisies.

Insects pollinate the daisies. Deer keep the daisy population under control.

It looks like everybody has an important job. We're all needed. And if some folks disappeared, the woods would change. What would happen if the possums disappeared?

Oh, my. Save the possums.

I'd forgotten that the woods need woodpeckers, squirrels, and possums to stay woodsy as well as insects, worms, bacteria, armadillos, and snakes.

I don't know whom else to thank. I don't even know whom else to google. Figuring out how all the animals and plants relate to each other in the woods behind my house is way beyond my ken.

Imagine trying to figure out how all the animals and plants

relate to each other on Planet Earth. All we know for sure is that our lives are seriously entangled. Humans might not do well if some folks disappeared. Since we have a lot of global power, we should probably make sure that our planet's mixed-species family does well.

That's how I view my household's mixed-species family. I have power over Cosmo, Kaylee, and Mary, so I take responsibility for their health. I honor their right to life, liberty, and happiness in the home we share.

They have their jobs to do, and I have mine. Mary alerts me whenever somebody walks by our house. Kaylee protects me from intruders, such as my guests. Cosmo entertains me. They all give me kisses. They make me a better person than I would have been had I not known them. In return, I give them food and lodging. Kisses too. Good deal.

Chapter 37

The Wild

YESTERDAY COSMO SCARED ME by disappearing for a while.

I was at "Betty Jean's desk" when I heard a crash somewhere in the house.

I jumped up from my computer and went in search of Cosmo. I looked in her room, where the shredded remains of a catalogue littered the floor; in my bedroom, where the shredded remains of a cardboard box littered the floor; in the laundry room, where puddles of water spotted the tiles; and in the kitchen, where all the cabinet doors were open. I still didn't find her.

I felt like I was following Hansel and Gretel.

Usually, when she's done something bad, Cosmo mutters, "No, no, bad bird," or, in a low voice, "Cosmooooooo." If she knows I'm looking for her, she calls out, "Here I am!"

I re-searched the house, opening every closet, every cabinet door. Finally, when I opened the cabinet door in my guest bathroom, I found her. She was perched atop the wastebasket being very still. Apparently, after she'd opened the cabinet door and climbed up on the wastebasket, the door had shut behind her, leaving her imprisoned in the dark. Since most birds, other than owls, stay quiet in the dark, Cosmo hadn't uttered a sound.

When I pulled her out, Cosmo said, "Hello," as if nothing untoward had happened. I kissed her.

after dark, in the wild it's not advantageous for birds to utter a sound. They don't want to alert nocturnal predators, such as owls, to their roost.

The incident caused me to ponder the force of instinct, which we think we've controlled in our own species. Cosmo surely heard me calling her name as I went through the house. Her culture, which she's acquired from me, must have made her want to respond "I'm here!" but her instinct made her stay quiet.

African grey parrots are not domesticated like dogs and cats. Our dogs and cats have descended from thousands of generations of dogs and cats bred to live with us humans and to serve us. Dogs are our best friends because we created them to love us. They are genetically tame.

Not so with our dear pet parrots who have descended from thousands of generations of wild parrots. Most of the greys we know had grandparents who flew through African rain forests, lived in large flocks, roosted in tall palms, ate palm nuts, berries, fruits, and seeds, and kept silent after nightfall. Parrots are still genetically wild.

One of Cosmo's Facebook friends, Jonathan Harris, explained this difference between dogs and parrots in another way. He said that dogs are genetically inclined to live in hierarchically organized packs whose members all obey the alpha dog. Thus dogs are naturally obedient. Wild parrots live in flocks that are not hierarchically organized. They have no alpha parrot, and they are not naturally obedient, although they do monitor and follow the actions of each other.

Cosmo never knew the wild, so she does not miss the rain forest. However tame she has become, though she still has the wild in her. Like all pet parrots—tamed but not domesticated—Cosmo would quickly revert to her wild nature if she did not have constant attention, care, and love.

By the way, in 2007, BirdLife International placed the African grey parrot on the IUCN Red List of Near Threatened Species. The IUCN, the International Union for Conservation of Nature—identifies species at risk for extinction and restricts their trade. The population of African greys is declining not only because of habitat loss but also because of their capture for trade.

People should never buy a wild-caught parrot. Not only

would they be breaking the law, but they would be guaranteeing an unhappy life for a bird who would always remember the freedom he or she had lost.

Cosmo is quite tame. She is cultured. But she still interprets anything unusual that happens to her from the standpoint of a wild bird. If I use a Dustbuster in her vicinity, she flies off her perch. If I carry a rake through her room on my way to the deck, she growls.

Now she is taking a "shower" in the dogs' water dish. She's exclaiming, "Wow, what a bird! Good shower!" She's calling, "I'm here! Come here!"

She is calling me not because she's like a human but because she's like a wild bird who wants to know where her mate is. She uses English because that's her means of communicating with me. If I were a bird, she'd chirp.

Chapter 38

Environmentalism

TONIGHT I HAD COSMO on my left hand—because she wouldn't get off—when I spotted a cockroach on my bedside table. It was little, but it was alive! I screamed: "¡Ay!" And jumped back.
Cosmo repeated: "¡Ay!" as she clung tightly to my hand.
The cockroach ran into the drawer. I groaned: "Oooooh."
Cosmo groaned: "Oooooh."
With my right hand, I grabbed a tissue fast as the speed of light, pinched the roach but not mortally, and chased it onto the floor. I stomped on it. I said, "Yuck!"
Cosmo said, "Do you wanna whistle?"
No, I wanted to gag, but since I try to do everything my bird requests, I whistled "*La Cucaracha*," a Mexican Mariachi song I learned as a little girl in El Paso. The lyrics are embedded in my memory:

> *La cucaracha, la cucaracha, ya no puede caminar*
> *Porque no tiene, porque le falta, una pata de atrás.*

> ("The cockroach, the cockroach, it can walk no more,
> Because it doesn't have, because it's missing, one of
> its hind legs.")

This incident shows that hard as I may try I'm not a biocentric egalitarian. A biocentric egalitarian believes that all organisms, including roaches, have equal worth.

I do know the importance to our biosphere of all its citizens: elk, eagles, sparrows, salamanders, guppies, groupers, kelp, kudzu, bees, bacteria, and roaches. But I kill roaches. Forgive me.

Even roaches have a job to do in nature. They're omnivores. They clean up the messes that nature's other diners make, and they serve as tasty food for scorpions, lizards, frogs, snakes, mice, and birds.

Biocentric egalitarianism is one environmentalist philosophy. Ecocentrism is another, a more holistic one. While the biocentric egalitarian acknowledges the right to life of every individual elk, sparrow, and roach, the ecocentrist focuses on the interactions of all of Earth's components, including water, soil, and air. In other words, the ecocentrist focuses on the whole. Both biocentrists and ecocentrists see humans as components of a larger ecosystem, not Earth's most important components. Both are dedicated environmentalists.

Then there is the anthropocentric—human-centric—environmentalist who campaigns for environmental health for the sake of us humans. I'm probably that kind of environmentalist.

I like contemplating the Earth as a wondrous ecosystem where the force of life courses through the veins of all of us interrelated, interacting residents. I don't want humans to cause any other species to go extinct. Nor do I want humans to go extinct either.

Toxic pollution and climate change could do both, in which case Earth would survive but without us and maybe without elks and sparrows. Probably with roaches, who have been scurrying around for three hundred fifty million years—that's one hundred fifty million years before dinosaurs and three hundred forty-seven million years before our human-ish ancestors.

Fortunately, if we anthropocentric environmentalists are to succeed in keeping Earth healthy for us, we will keep it healthy for all our planet's residents. And if we try to keep all of our planet's residents healthy, we keep ourselves healthy. It works both ways. We live together.

In the nineteenth-century coal mines, the caged canary's job was to die in the presence of noxious gases and thereby alert the miners to get out of the tunnels. They were the nineteenth-century smoke alarms. As I bird-lover, I'm sad for those unfortunate canaries.

If we think of all Earth's species as miners' canaries, then we'll interpret the disappearance of a species as a warning that our own species may be getting into trouble.

Lately if I come home after dark, Cosmo calls out "beep beep beep beep beep" till I let her out of her cage. She sounds like a truck's back-up warning. Now why would Cosmo do that at the end of the day? Because that's what she's heard during the day. She's a parrot.

I pay attention to every sound Cosmo makes, not just because she's adorably funny—she is—but because she reflects what's happening around us that I may not have noticed. She lets me know that the smoke alarm needs new batteries by mimicking their pip pip pip. She lets me know that someone's left a message on the answering machine by mimicking the caller's voice. She lets me know when crows have visited. "Caw caw."

I learn from Cosmo. I use what I learn to make our environment healthier and more pleasurable for both of us. We're partners because we live together and influence each other.

CHAPTER 39

Eyesight

"THAT'S BIRDIE," Cosmo will tell me, gazing at whatever doves, finches, chickadees, woodpeckers, cardinals, crows, and blue jays are eating seed off the deck railing. Then, at the arrival of a few squirrels, she'll add, "Look! Squirrel!"

Cosmo is calling my attention to the ruckus outdoors. Apparently, she wants me to see what she sees.

Although the birds and the squirrels are numerous and boisterous, engaged in activity that far exceeds anybody's vocabulary to describe, I reply, "Yes, that's birdie," or, "That's squirrel."

Then Cosmo might say, "Cosmo is a birdy," associating herself with both the crow and the chickadee. In my interpretation of her utterances, Cosmo confirms her knowledge of birds when she says, "Birdie has feathers."

I have to remind myself that the simplicity of Cosmo's speech does not at all represent any simplicity of thought. Cosmo's thought must be profoundly more sophisticated than she reveals in the limited English vocabulary she uses.

If Cosmo sees the same visually complex world humans see, she too must have complex thoughts she can't put into words.

Actually, Cosmo sees much that humans *don't* see. Birds have cones in the retina of the eye that enable them to see colors in the ultraviolet range invisible to us. Cosmo's vision is far superior to mine in the daytime.

Not even all birds see the world the same way. Diurnal birds, active during the day, see more colors at the ultraviolet end of the spectrum and therefore see best in the daytime. Nocturnal birds, like owls, see more colors at the infrared end and see best at night. Some birds don't see in the dark at all, and for that reason stay very still after nightfall.

The Fourth of July is coming up. I wonder whether whole flocks of sleeping diurnal birds will panic at the sound of fireworks and fly blindly into trees, buildings, and power lines, as they did one year in Georgia and Arkansas.

The world is full of colors that some animals see and others don't. Bird feathers may reflect ultraviolet light that enables other birds to recognize their gender. I needed a DNA test to find out that Cosmo was a female.

I've learned that the urine and feces of mice have ultraviolet colors that their avian predators see and that their human predators don't. I love thinking that mice leave behind some really beautiful poop—beautiful, that is, from a raptor's perspective—as they scurry through amber fields of grain.

Scientists studying the eyesight of other species have determined that eagles see at least four times better than humans because their retinas have many more cones; that squirrels see through yellow-tinted eye lenses, like sun-glasses; and that dogs see the world mostly in shades of violet, blue, and gray.

Contemplate trillions of animals—birds, squirrels, dogs, horses, deer, sharks, snakes, bumblebees, ants, and humans—all seeing things differently from each other. Or perhaps ech sees different things. I guess the world is as it seems to the individual observer.

I wonder what I look like to Cosmo. What does she see in me that my human friends don't? I'll bet she sees an ultraviolet halo.

I don't know what animal's world looks like any more than a blind person knows what a seeing person's world looks like.

I don't know what Cosmo thinks about when she looks at birds, squirrels, trees, and carpenter bees. What does she think about when the rain beats its rainy rhythm on the skylight of her room? What does she think about when the squirrels land with a thump on her roof? What does she think about when she waits in her cage for me to come home to let her out?

She must think about things not immediately visible to her.

Cosmo is back in her cage now because I'm about to leave the house and I don't want her to disappear into the recesses of the towel cabinet where I can't reach her. We have been whistling duets, mostly a not-for-recording version of "Bridge on the River Kwai." Periodically she pauses to call out to a crow, "Caw caw," or to a dove or a cardinal. Periodically she announces loudly, "I'm here!" in case I've forgotten.

Just now Mary raced out through the doggy door, barking loudly and bringing chaos to the congregation of feathery and furry creatures.

"Mary doggie bark," Cosmo observed for my benefit.

That's what Cosmo said, but what did she think when she saw the birds take flight and the squirrels leap through the air—in colors foreign to me?

CHAPTER 40

Zoos

COSMO WAS SOOOO BAD tonight! She was perched on her T-stand in the dining room foraging in her food dish. Although she had no way down she was happy because she was not behind bars. She was accompanying Harry Belafonte with her whistling. "Day-O."

But Cosmo must have gotten bored watching me cook. Suddenly, with great glee, she flung her peanuts, cashews, and parrot pellets one by one across the kitchen. Every time I chased down a pellet, she tossed another one my way. And laughed hysterically.

Of course my dogs Kaylee and Mary scarfed up most of those pellets, cashews, and peanuts, so I didn't need to get out the broom.

I removed the food dish from the T-stand. Cosmo immediately hurried to the water dish, dipped herself in it, splashed around, climbed out, flapped her wings, and sent a million droplets of water across the dining room.

I yelled, "Cosmoooo!"

"Cosmoooo" She mocked me and chuckled.

According to what I've read, Cosmo's fun-with-food behavior is typical of a parrot, at least of a normal, contented parrot. But many parrots get locked up for doing what comes naturally.

I was thinking of the life of caged birds when I visited Zoo Atlanta for the first time. I recommend Zoo Atlanta to everybody. It's attractive, educational, entertaining, and clean.

I saw birds who had never alighted on my deck railing: a four-foot-high male kori bustard weighing about thirty-five pounds, perhaps the heaviest flighted bird in the world; a

Cassowary, probably the second heaviest; an ostrich; a wreathed hornbill; a Bali mynah; a flock of Chilean flamingos; hundreds of gorgeous budgerigars.

My favorite mammals in Zoo Atlanta were the gorillas, who live on a two-acre tract that includes five different habitats. The gorillas all have names, as is appropriate. They are unique individuals with unique faces, unique nose prints, unique personalities. Like humans. They seem happy. They roam all over the zoo's Ford African Rain Forest. They have families, with babies.

Humans have collected wild animals for five thousand years. The civilizations of ancient Egypt, China, and Mesopotamia had menageries. By the fourth century BCE, the big city-states in Greece had zoos. By the late eighteenth century, Vienna, Madrid, and Paris had zoos.

Until recently the mission of zoos was to display exotic animals. Lions, tigers, elephants and gorillas paced back and forth in cages or enclosures designed for humans' viewing pleasure and intellectual enlightenment, not theirs.

But in the 1970s, the mission of zoos started changing, and so did their architecture. Our understanding of the relationship of humans to the rest of nature was changing. Do you remember what was going on in Britain and the United States then?

Environmentalists were examining the effect of habitat on health, humans' health and everybody else's. Ecologists warned of species extinctions. Animal behaviorists discovered ways that great apes, dolphins, and birds communicate with each other. Washoe the chimpanzee and Koko the gorilla learned American Sign Language.

In 1970, Oxford psychologist Richard Ryder coined the term *speciesists* for humans who treated other animals as inferiors, and in 1975 Peter Singer published the book *Animal Liberation.*

Now, in the twenty-first century, the mission of zoos as set forth by the Association of Zoos and Aquariums (AZA) is fourfold: conservation of species, education, scientific research, and recreation. The happiness of the zoos' residents matters.

What's happened since 1970? We humans have expanded our ethical community to include non-human animals. The passage of animal protection laws is evidence of our change of heart.

I know. We still have a long way to go.

As you know, I think of Cosmo as a feathery little person, a member of my family, whom I don't keep locked up. I give her freedom to explore my house when I'm home.

Maybe that's why I'm always finding stuff in odd places: a pan the kitchen floor; a comb on the bathroom floor; the contents of an overturned wastebasket on the bedroom floor.

"Cosmo, where are you?"

CHAPTER 41

More and Less

THIS MORNING AS I PUT on nail polish at my bathroom counter I glanced down to see Cosmo stealthily opening the bottom drawer. Cosmo looked up to see whether I'd noticed. I gently shut the drawer, and went back to my nails. She opened it again. I shut it again. Then she yanked it wide open and immediately climbed in. She chuckled.

I gave her a lift into her cage.

As soon as her cage door closed, Cosmo begged to be let out: "Cosmo wanna go up. Cosmo be a good bird. Cosmo don't bite. I love you. Betty Jean wanna kiss? Smooch smooch smooch smooch smooch. That's four kiss."

I let her but first I corrected her arithmetic: "Four kiss. Smooch smooch smooch smooch. That's four kiss."

I had initiated Cosmo's formal education a few years ago after I'd learned from Irene Pepperberg's book *Alex and Me* that Alex could count to six. Since Cosmo is an African grey parrot like Alex, I figured I'd teach Cosmo to count too. No success. Cosmo interpreted "four" to mean "many."

Cosmo has since dropped out of school.

Last May University of Rochester researchers reported in the journal *Frontiers in Psychology* that baboons can tell the difference between many peanuts and few peanuts but can't count. The researchers put unequal numbers of peanuts in paper cups and then watched eight baboons select the cup with the most peanuts. When the difference between the numbers was big, the baboons selected the larger amount more frequently than when the difference was small.

The Rochester researchers concluded that baboons can't keep track of discrete objects the way humans do but that they "can show you that five is more than two."

To me the Rochester researchers proved only that baboons know the difference between "more" and "less." What in baboons' evolutionary history would prepare them to count anyway?

I mention the Rochester study for two reasons. It indicates that researchers are earnestly seeking evidence that non-human animals are smart, in keeping with our fairly recent recognition that humans are not unique in our cognitive abilities. Good. But it also shows that we tend to judge everybody's intelligence on the ability or inability to measure up to our human standards. Not so good.

I believe that baboons and other animals can't count peanuts or anything else because they don't have a language with an embedded numerical system. We humans can keep track of twelve peanuts because we can say "one two three four five six seven eight nine ten eleven twelve." We have names for all those numbers. And we have a system that enables us to count to thirteen million if we have the time and the desire. I don't.

By having names for numbers, humans can add, subtract, multiply, divide, and do complex calculations. We can keep track of discrete objects, even objects as small as particles of pollen and grains of sand, even objects as invisible to the naked eye as neutrons and distant stars, even objects as intangible as stocks and bonds. We can think of numbers abstractly, theoretically, unrepresentative of things.

Consequently, we can discover the laws of physics and create weapons of mass destruction. We can manufacture planes, trains, and automobiles, telescopes, microscopes, and cameras. We can create money, save it in the bank, and count it.

If humans didn't have language, I suspect we'd see the world the way baboons see the world: big pile of peanuts better than little pile of peanuts rather than thirty-six peanuts better than twenty-four peanuts.

Humans are very different from the rest of the animal kingdom in what we can create and discover. Our language makes us so.

I said earlier that Cosmo can't count. But she does know the difference between more and less in a realm beyond peanuts. Cosmo will ask me, "Betty Jean wanna whistle?" And then she'll whistle "Whee whew."

I'll whistle "Whee whee whew."

Cosmo will whistle "Whee whee whee whew."

I'll whistle "Whee whee whee whee whew."

Then Cosmo will whistle "Whee whee whee whee whee whee whee whee whee whee whew!"

Cosmo knows she's won the counting game.

CHAPTER 42

Scented Breath

COSMO HAS PEANUT BREATH.

I don't know why Cosmo's peanut breath surprised me. She'd been eating peanuts. We know that humans have peppermint breath after eating breath mints, garlic breath after eating gazpacho, and bourbon breath after drinking an Old Fashioned.

We are well aware of the breath of our dogs and cats and ferrets. We can imagine the breath of lions, who eat gazelles, and koalas, who eat eucalyptus leaves. And snakes, who eat mice. Snakes must have mouse breath. Mice must have grain breath.

But birds? Just think: Every single bird in the world including finches, robins, doves, kingfishers, vultures, and macaws has scented breath. Even the tiniest bird in the world, the bee hummingbird, which weighs .063 ounces, has scented breath. Nectar-scented breath.

I suspect that a kingfisher's breath gives off the scent of fish, a vulture's breath the scent of dead squirrel.

Cosmo's wild cousins in Africa probably have insect breath. We breathe what we eat.

The Latin word for "breath" is spiritus, which is the origin of the English word "spirit." And the Latin word for the verb "to breathe" is spirare. Inspirare means "to breathe or blow into," and also "to inspire," in the sense of imparting a truth to someone. For the ancient Greeks and Romans, the gods breathe spirit into individuals, "inspiring" them to create poetry and music and to do good deeds. For Christians, God breathes life into all Creation through the Holy Spirit.

We can see the connection between breath and spirit when

we think of our words "respiration," the act of breathing, and "expiration," the act of dying. A dictionary meaning of expire is "to breathe one's last breath."

Everybody's got breath—that is, everybody who is alive—so everybody's got spirit.

I love thinking about Cosmo's spirit.

All of Earth's creatures breathe the same air. It's like we're in an airplane, but with more air. And trees. Trees respire, too. We are interrelated and interdependent. We are family.

I hope our planet doesn't get bad breath. It would affect the spirit of all our planet's inhabitants. Maybe we humans can keep that from happening.

Do humans and other animals kiss each other on the lips—or beak or snout—because that's where the other's breath is? Why do we do that when some of us have peanut breath and others of us have garlic breath? We kiss instinctively, without regard to the scent of the breath.

Kissing must be a spirit-to-spirit thing.

Since it's an expression of affection, kissing shows a desire for knowing the other's spirit. Or breath. Whatever.

Cosmo certainly associates kissing with affection. When she was reunited with her clutch mate at the pet store, after two months apart, the two of them rushed to kiss each other. They put their little black tongues into each other's beak. Now how much fun was that, unless it was spirit-to-spirit communication?

Cosmo often tells me, "Cosmo wanna kiss," and puts her warm beak out for me to kiss it. Sometimes she says, "Cosmo wanna kiss on the beak." Sometimes she asks, "Betty Jean wanna kiss feathers?" She'll usually follow the kiss with "I love you" or "Cosmo wanna cuddle."

But Cosmo can be wily. Yesterday, an acquaintance of ours came over to meet Cosmo. I put Cosmo on her arm. Cosmo looked at her and said, "Cosmo wanna kiss!"

The woman asked me uneasily, "What should I do? She wants a kiss!"

I advised her, "Decline."

I could tell what Cosmo was up to. I knew from experience. One morning before I was able to read her body language, Cosmo said to me, "Cosmo wanna kiss!" I leaned over to kiss her, and she bit me! I had to teach class with a big welt on my upper lip. I didn't explain.

CHAPTER 43

Keeping a Beat

COSMO BRUSHES HER BEAK while I brush my teeth.

Let me explain. Yesterday when I wasn't paying attention to her, Cosmo went into my cosmetic drawer, which is her favorite place to investigate—opened it fully, and hid in the recess behind it. To retrieve her, I had to pull the drawer completely out of the cabinet. That was tiresome. Once I got her on my hand I parked her on the chrome towel rack by the sink to keep her in my range of vision and out of trouble.

I proceeded to brush my teeth. Then I looked up at Cosmo.

Cosmo was watching me and brushing her beak back and forth on the towel rack with my rhythm.

She brushed with me again today.

Cosmo's mimicry of my brushing surprised me because she has never mimicked my actions before, to my knowledge.

However, Cosmo's mimicry would not surprise Irena Schulz, rescuer of the now famous male Sulphur-crested cockatoo named Snowball. Snowball dances to the song "Everybody" of the Backstreet Boys. You can watch him and other dancing parrots on YouTube.

Snowball had learned to dance probably by mimicking his previous humans, who must have really, really liked the Backstreet Boys. But Snowball captured the attention of researchers not by his fine mimicry but by his excellent rhythm. Snowball bobs his head, sways back and forth, and stomps his feet to the beat of the music.

Aniruddh D. Patel, author of the book *Music, Language, and the Brain,* and John R. Iversen of the Neurosciences Institute in La Jolla saw Snowball's YouTube video and decided to study the bird's ability to keep a beat. They tested Snowball outside the presence of human dancers to rule out mimicry. Through digital recordings they found that Snowball was synchronizing his body movements to the music and that he was dancing on his own.

In a 2008 article, they wrote that Snowball was the first non-human animal proven to have "beat perception."

Patel believes that only the animals capable of complex vocal learning, such as parrots, songbirds, and dolphins, are physiologically able to perceive a musical beat and synchronize their body movements to it. The highly intelligent chimpanzees and gorillas cannot, because they are physiologically incapable of complex vocal learning.

Humans, parrots, songbirds, and dolphins are all in the same prestigious category of complex vocal learners capable of keeping time to music. We are the singers and dancers of the universe!

Would cockatoos dance in the wild? Not to music, of course, because, supposedly, music is made only by humans. At least, human kind of music is made by humans, such as Beethoven's Ninth, "Blowing in the Wind," "*La Cucaracha*," and "Everybody."

Patel and Iversen do not consider the rhythmic chorus of tree frogs and crickets calling back and forth, beautiful as it is, to be music. They consider it a "pulse train," or pulse wave.

Snowball's love of dancing must be an acquired taste for him. It is an aspect of his culture, not his nature, although he was naturally equipped to develop dancing skills.

Because wild cockatoos, like wild African greys, stay with their parents for up to two years, they have a long learning period. Because they are gregarious, in need of the company of others, the parrots learn from their flock mates. I think that's why domestically raised parrots can acquire the speech and culture of their humans.

This afternoon Cosmo and I watched Snowball dance. Cosmo said excitedly, "That's birdie!" and "That's a bird!"

Cosmo loves to watch animals on the computer, which she calls "television."

So I googled David Attenborough's YouTube video of a superb lyre bird. The superb lyre bird is a two-pound, thirty-five-inch-long, ground-dwelling Australian bird known for his extraordinary mimicry. The male was mimicking not only the calls of other birds in the forest, but also the sounds of a camera shutter, a car alarm, and a chainsaw. He was recording the destruction of his habitat.

Cosmo watched in fascination. "That's birdie!" she exclaimed. And she whistled to the image on the screen: "Whee whew!" Cosmo recognized the Superb Lyre bird as a bird even though she'd never seen a bird of that size or shape.

Then came an advertisement for cat food, and a cat appeared on screen. Cosmo asked, "What's that?"

CHAPTER 44

Talking with Animals

COSMO LOVES TO CONVERSE with me. Her longest sentence to date is: "Time for shower for Cosmo in Cosmo room." That was in response to my taking a shower before accommodating her wishes.

Humans have a history of wanting to talk with animals. In the last fifty years, many Doctor Doolittle wannabes have turned their curiosity about animal intelligence into scientific investigation that has fundamentally transformed our understanding of our fellow residents of Earth.

Pioneers of the field worked with great apes.

In the late 1960s Beatrix and Allen Gardner taught American Sign Language to a young, wild-caught chimpanzee named Washoe. Over her lifetime, spent for the most part at the Chimpanzee and Human Communication Institute at Central Washington University, Washoe acquired a vocabulary of three hundred fifty ASL words and taught many of them to her adopted son Loulis.

In the 1970s, Francine Patterson, a PhD student in psychology at Stanford University, began teaching American Sign Language to a young female lowland gorilla named Koko. Before her death, Koko used one thousand ASL signs and understood two thousand words in spoken English. Like Cosmo, Koko put the words together in novel ways to communicate.

In the 1970s, Duane and Sue Rumbaugh and my late, dear friend Ernst von Glasersfeld developed a system of lexigrams for communication with a young chimpanzee named Lana at the Yerkes Regional Primate Research Center at Emory University. Using an electronic keyboard connected to a computer, Lana touched the lexigrams on the screen to express her wishes: "banana," "Tim tickle Lana," etc. Lana could even question her trainer Tim about what he had put in the "machine."

In the 1980s, critics of the researchers' linguistic claims said that the apes weren't using grammar. But I remember thinking "So what?" I had a picture of Koko on my office door at the time, and I'd become one of Koko's fans. I cared about what Koko had accomplished, not what she hadn't.

To really appreciate Koko's accomplishment, imagine being dropped as a child into the jungle of central Africa and left in the care of a troop of lowland gorillas. You had to learn their complex system of grunts, barks, belches, screeches, and roars—for that's what their calls sounded like to you—if you wanted to communicate your needs. By the age of twenty-five, you had learned twenty-five different calls. You didn't know gorilla grammar, but you got along okay.

You weren't a gorilla. You knew it, and so did all the gorillas. But since you had no human companions, you tried your best to fit into gorilla society. After all, you depended on your gorilla companions for food, lodging, and affection. You wanted your gorilla companions to treat you as well as they treated each other, even though you weren't very hairy and couldn't swing through trees.

Washoe, Koko, and Lana, through no desire of their own, occupied the same position in our human society. Their accomplishments led in 1994 to the Great Ape Project, which aims to "include the non-human great apes within the community of equals by granting them the basic moral and legal protections that only humans currently enjoy." These unusual great apes changed our view of primates' intelligence fundamentally.

I think that Alex, the African grey whom Irene Pepperberg studied, has changed our view of parrots' intelligence fundamentally.

This afternoon I was reading in Cosmo's room. From atop her cage Cosmo asked, "Wanna cuddle?"

I responded, with my eyes on my book—*Spain: A Culinary Road Trip*, by Mario Batali with Gwyneth Paltrow—"I'm busy."

Cosmo repeated, "I wanna cuddle!"

I murmured, "Just a minute, Cosmo."

Cosmo then said, "Cosmo wanna cuddle! Please!"

I complied.

CHAPTER 45

Cambridge Declaration on Consciousness

COSMO IS WHISTLING the Meow Mix tune. Remember it? "Meow meow meow meow, meow meow meow meow . . ." and so on.

Cosmo got the tune from me. I was whistling it one evening without realizing where I'd heard it.

Cosmo is now perched atop her tall cage behind me as I write. She's incorporated "Meow Mix" into a minute-long original composition with fragments of "*Heigh-Ho*," "Wooden Heart," and "Yankee Doodle," various warbles, trills, bird calls, and barks she has picked up from her human, avian, and canine friends, and some bars of music I've never heard before and will never hear again.

Cosmo has just paused to congratulate herself. "Wow, whatta bird!" She's evidently pleased with her vocal creation.

Cosmo is whistling for the sheer delight of it. She's not calling to a mate. She's not mimicking me. She has no purpose in her whistling beyond self-entertainment. She's expressing her joy in life. But isn't that why we humans whistle?

Cosmo does behave a lot like us.

Humans used to believe that we alone in the universe had "consciousness." Well, I didn't really think that, but most learned people did. To them, consciousness was what humans had that even the smartest parrots, dogs, dolphins, gorillas, and elephants did not have.

Now some very learned people are acknowledging that we humans have been wrong.

On July 7, 2012, a group of prominent neuroscientists at an international conference in England on "Consciousness in Human and non-Human Animals" signed a "Cambridge

Declaration on Consciousness." It said:

> ... the weight of evidence indicates that humans are not unique in possessing the neurological substrates that generate consciousness. Non-human animals, including all mammals and birds, and many other creatures, including octopuses, also possess these neurological substrates.

This means that the brains of humans and non-human animals are not as different from each other as we had supposed. It's official.

Official, but not surprising, at least not to pet lovers. Anybody who loves a dog or a cat or a bird would not be a bit surprised to learn that our pets' minds are similar to our own.

However, the Cambridge Declaration on Consciousness is actually a big deal, a really, really big deal. It will have consequences for our whole society.

In many medical laboratories, factory farms, zoos, and pet stores, we've treated non-human animals without much respect because we assumed those animals lack the feelings we humans possess. We considered ourselves superior to everybody else because we had consciousness. So we felt justified in subjecting everybody else to our wishes.

With the Cambridge Declaration that everybody, or almost everybody, has consciousness, our society will be morally obligated to treat non-human animals more kindly.

What's "consciousness" anyway? I figure it's a modern-day version of "soul," by which we've historically differentiated humans from other animals.

Back to Cosmo, who is now practicing "Meow Mix" with my assistance. We're doing a duet. She whistles the first part, and I finish up. That's how she learns a tune, from beginning to end.

Each time we conclude a duet, Cosmo whistles a brand new, wild and wonderful composition. I wonder: When she whistles all over the scale, does Cosmo think she's making beautiful music? She seems to take pride in her accomplishment. Is Cosmo an artist?

Or is art uniquely human? Do we say that if humans create a melody it's art, but if a parrot creates a melody it's not art? Seems like we do.

CHAPTER 46

Accents

ONE MORNING NOT LONG AGO I awoke to the extremely loud call of a Northern cardinal. It sounded as if the bird were in my house. Well, a bird was, but not a cardinal. Cosmo was spiritedly mimicking the wild avian inhabitants of our woods.

I heard: "purdy purdy purdy whoit whoit whoit whoit," the cardinal. Then, "oo-wah-hooo, hoo-hoo," a mourning dove. Then "peter peter peter," a tufted titmouse. The sounds of nature.

How lovely.

Then "Beep beep beep beep beep." Whoa! What was that? Oh yes, a truck backing up.

Finally I heard, in my voice, "I'm here! Come here! Cosmo wanna go up!" I got up and let Cosmo out of her cage.

Cosmo is a superb mimic. She must have superb hearing.

Birds' hearing is generally much more acute than human hearing. Some researchers describe it as "more detailed." Birds can distinguish sounds from each other that blend together for humans unless we record and analyze them electronically. They can discriminate not only a huge variety of calls from different birds, but also different calls from the same bird.

Cosmo fooled me into thinking I had a cardinal in my house, but she probably didn't fool the cardinal's mate. And she probably didn't understand what the cardinal was saying to his mate.

The Northern cardinal has some sixteen different calls for different purposes — such as locating his mate, sounding an alarm, for warning intruders on his territory, etc. Cosmo would not have understood the calls.

By the way, according to the Cornell Lab of Ornithology, cardinals have regional accents,

Like humans.

Like parrots. Every African grey family has its own accent. And every African grey flock has its own accent. Biologist Michael Schindlinger says flocks of parrots develop their own dialect because young parrots mimic the calls of the other flock members.

Grey babies have a lengthy learning period. They don't reach sexual maturity until they are six years old, on average. In their first year, when they stay close to their parents, the fledglings learn their calls from their parents and the rest of their flock. They are not born knowing how to how to make a specific chirp as we have learned from digital recordings, each family has its own accent.

Whale pods too have their unique accent. Whales communicate with a system of vocal signals, and whales in different regions of the ocean have different dialects. The enormous blue whales, who vocalize at frequencies too low for humans to hear, use sound to navigate, find a mate, and alert each other about food sources. Their signals can travel a thousand miles through the water. When the male and female whales get together, they may discover they have different accents.

Crows, almost universally exalted for their high intelligence, vary their calls according to what they want to say. They have calls to signal alarm, distress, and the desire to get together.

And crows from different regions have different accents..

Those who have regional accents must do some learning from each other. And they must hear very well.

Even prairie dogs talk with each other and have regional dialects. Con Slobodchikoff of Northern Arizona University and his students decoded the alarm calls of Gunnison's prairie dogs and found that the prairie dogs emit different alarm calls for different predators, such as coyotes, dogs, hawks, and humans. The prairie dogs even vary their alarm calls to give physical descriptions of the predators. Slobodchikoff claims that their calls are like short sentences made of nouns and adjectives.

Researchers have recently discovered that every single animal on our planet has a unique voice. By studying sound spectrographs of their calls, researchers have concluded that many, many animals, both avian and mammalian, have different calls appropriate to different situations.

Everybody's talking! And humans used to think we were the only ones.

But can the birds hear each other over the sound of trucks?

Can the whales hear each other over the sound of cruise ships, cargo ships, submarines, and aircraft carriers? If they can't, how will they ever find mates?

Noise pollution doesn't stop humans from making babies, but it may stop some of our planet's other communicative creatures.

To Cosmo, the sound of a truck backing up is not noise pollution. The truck's beeps, as well as the other sounds we industrious humans make with our machines, are noise pollution only to those of us who can remember or can imagine a time or a place without trucks, trains, ships, or planes.

Does a ninety-year-old Blue whale remember a time when he heard no ships?

For Cosmo, hatched in 2001, the sound of a truck is as normal a part of her world as the sound of a cardinal.

It's time for Cosmo to go to bed. After spending an hour speaking enthusiastically about feathers, fur, doggies, and birdies, interrupting her own monologue with barks and hoots and beeps and cheeps, quiet chuckles, and raucous laughs, Cosmo just told me, "Cosmo wanna cuddle. Cosmo wanna go to bed!"

But as I approached her, she raised her left foot and asked, "Betty Jean wanna kiss feet?"

I let her wrap her four toes around my nose. She chuckled. "Hehehehe." Then with her beak she yanked an earring off my left ear.

Chapter 47

Dawn Chorus

Cosmo has a recorded vocabulary of over one hundred sixty-five words and innumerable novel utterances.

But can Cosmo talk to other talkative African grey parrots? I'm often asked that question.

I suppose that African greys who are raised with the same vocabulary could communicate with each other in human language. But that situation would be unusual because different humans are likely to use different vocabulary in speaking to their birds. Nobody speaks like Cosmo.

I say to Cosmo, "Cosmo wanna go in a car?" Another human may say to her parrot, "Georgie, shall we take a ride?" The two birds would not understand each other. It would be as if each found the other to be speaking a foreign language.

Most of the pet African greys in the world do speak a foreign language. African greys in Mexico speak Spanish. African Greys in Holland speak Dutch. african greys in Japan speak Japanese. You can listen to them on YouTube.

As we know from sonograms, even wild birds may not understand their relatives in distant geographical regions because of slight differences in their calls that only birds can detect.

In the woods of Georgia, Michigan, Colorado, and Oregon, the dawn chorus of birds includes the American crow. But the crow is not playing the same exact notes in Georgia, Michigan, Colorado, and Oregon, at least not to the ear of another crow.

In fact, the dawn chorus is unique everywhere in the world, for everywhere, even in ecosystems that resemble each other, its music is produced by a unique configuration of birds. No two choruses are ever the same, not in space, not in time.

A few months ago, Cosmo and I were invited to the home of friends of mine who live a couple of miles away from my house. We sat on the porch, drank wine, talked, and enjoyed the chirping of the birds. Cosmo paid rapt attention, not to us but to the birds. She was listening to a chorus she hadn't heard before.

What did Cosmo hear that we did not? A symphony of wondrous sounds far more interesting to her than our conversation, an unrepeatable avian concert that humans are not aurally equipped to hear fully.

Although birders are no better equipped aurally than the rest of us bird-loving humans, they are much better listeners of avian concerts and far more knowledgeable about what they do hear. They have what I say is a magnificent obsession: to identify the birds who sing for each other in the forests, deserts, plains, and mountains of all seven continents.

However, these dedicated birders will probably not hear as many birds as their grandparents did, even if they follow in their grandparents' footsteps, even if they go to parks and preserves where the government protects wildlife, even if they trek through wilderness.

Before long they might not hear the wood thrush. The Wood thrush, whose melodious song has graced our Southeastern woodlands for centuries, has decreased in number by fifty percent since the 1960s because of loss of breeding grounds.

Out of curiosity I played a recording of a wood thrush on the Cornell Lab of Ornithology. Cosmo asked, "What's that?" and promptly exclaimed delightedly, "That's birdie!"

In 2020, Aylin Woodward reported a twenty-nine percent decline since 1970 in the number of birds in North America, amounting to three billion birds. Because of climate change and habitat loss, two thirds of North American bird species are at risk of extinction. Among the endangered bird species are hawks, hummingbirds, jays, owls, wrens, and parrots, particularly macaws and amazons.

Will our symphony of bird songs turn into a quartet?

David Yarnold, president and CEO of the National Audubon Society wrote that "This is a bird emergency with a clear message: the natural world humans depend on is being paved, logged, eroded and polluted. You don't need to look hard for the metaphor: birds are the canaries in the coal mine that is the earth's future."

I occasionally listen to CDs as I write in the evening. But tonight after ten minutes of Samuel Barber's "Adagio for Strings," I realized I was ignoring Cosmo's musical tastes. She was perched on her cage behind me, preening and waiting patiently—or rather, impatiently—for me to notice her. I went back to the Cornell Lab for other bird songs. Together we enjoyed the sounds of cardinals, owls, doves, ducks, and loons.

Cosmo has never heard a loon. We don't live near a lake. "What's that?" she asked.

Then, suddenly bored with the loon, Cosmo climbed down, waddled down the hall, and said out loud but to herself, "Cosmo wanna shower."

CHAPTER 48

Crows

YESTERDAY COSMO OPENED AND DISAPPEARED into one of my kitchen cabinets. I knew she'd gone into the liquor cabinet but I nevertheless called out, "Cosmo, where are you?"

"Cosmo are here!" she answered.

So while Cosmo explored the Jack Daniels whiskey and the Craigellachie scotch, I took out the garbage. When I came back into the house, Cosmo was hurrying down the hall toward me. "There you are!" she exclaimed. She doesn't like me to leave without telling her.

Cosmo followed me back to the kitchen, commenting "Look, birdies," as she passed the sliding glass door to the deck. She called out to the crows, "Caw caw."

Over the past years I've grown accustomed to being followed around the house by a self-confident, sixteen-ounce, six-inch-tall feathery little person who talks like me and walks like a pigeon.

Since the crows—six of them in total—began visiting my deck railing, I've been reading about the species. I've learned that crows mate for life, share parental responsibilities, use tools, solve problems, play elaborate social games with each other, trick other birds out of their food, recognize human faces, and have long memories. A group of crows is called a "murder," not a flock.

Crows belong to the corvid family, which also includes ravens, magpies, and jays, all of them smart, sociable, and playful. They have a brain-to-body weight ratio equal to great apes and parrots and only slightly lower than humans. This encephalization quotient indicates to researchers that as a species crows are among Earth's most intelligent animals.

In his book *Gifts of the Crow,* University of Washington wild-life biologist John Marzluff tells of banding a crow he named Light Blue, Dark Blue. Over the next seven years, Light Blue, Dark Blue became friendly with John's neighbors but not with John. The crow never forgave John for applying the light blue and dark blue anklets, and he expressed his anger by follow-ing John every time he spied him, scolding him with loud caws, leading fellow crows to treat him similarly, and generally threatening him.

Lately I've been thinking that if crows can distinguish us humans from each other, humans ought to be able to recognize individual crows. Yet because we usually don't name crows, or any of the other wild animals whom we watch, we don't think of them as individuals. So I've decided to name the six members of our neighborhood's murder of crows.

There's Methuselah, who looks old because his neck feathers are always in disarray. According to the Bible, Methuselah lived to be nine hundred and sixty-nine years old. Grip, after Charles Dickens's pet raven, who became the subject of Edgar Allen Poe's long poem "The Raven." Then Nevermore, which is what Edgar Allen Poe's raven said. "Quoth the raven, Nevermore. And Aesop, "Cheryl," and Russell.

If two more crows join the murder, I'll name them José Cuervo and Old Crow 80 Proof.

I'll bet if we named every wild animal we spotted, we'd be better keepers of their habitat. We'd want our non-human friends' homes to be clean and toxin-free so they could raise healthy families.

At four o'clock this morning I awoke to hear my dogs barking furiously in the back yard. I went out on the deck and saw a raccoon sitting precariously atop a tall tree stump just out of the dogs' reach. As soon as I thought of her as Mrs. Raccoon, I realized how scared she must have been and how grateful to see me when I lured the dogs back inside with cheese.

I wonder whether Mrs. Raccoon had brought her babies— let's call them Bonnie, Clyde, and Lone Ranger—for dinner at my railing. They might have been hiding in the tree.

Did you know that federal law does not allow us to keep crows, or any other member of the Corvid family native to the United States, as pets? Federal law does permit licensed hunters to shoot and kill crows except during peak nesting season. It permits unlicensed individuals to shoot and kill crows "committing, or about to commit, depredations on agricultural crops, or when concentrated in such numbers and manner as to constitute a health hazard or other nuisance." I guess the government protects crows during peak nesting season to make more crows for people to shoot.

My neighbors Jim and Nelle told me that some crows—I presume they were referring to Methuselah, Grip, Nevermore, Aesop, Cheryl, and Russell—had dug up the colorful labels on their recently planted hellebores and transported the labels to the bird bath. I'm happy to report that Jim did not blast the mischief makers into crow heaven with an AK-47 but instead admired their newly decorated bird bath.

CHAPTER 49

Rat Snake

ONE SUMMER EVENING Cosmo, Kaylee, Mary, and I had an adventure with a big snake.

Cosmo and I were in the study. I had been writing and chatting with her, and she had been whistling and chatting with me. She had just hopped onto my hand.

Suddenly Mary interrupted our bliss with fierce barking, much fiercer than her usual signal that a dog has walked down our street. I raced into the bedroom, parked Cosmo on top of the cage there, and went out onto the deck to find Mary in a stand-off with a very scary black-and-tweed snake. The snake was curled up in the corner against the house and flicking its snaky little tongue in and out of its mouth to try to frighten Mary.

Oh, no! I thought. The snake is going to kill Mary now, then slither into the house and kill Kaylee, hide until my bedtime and slither into my bed and kill me, and finally slither into Cosmo's room, slither up her cage, and kill Cosmo.

What an incident for the *Athens Banner Herald's* "Police Blotter"! The headline would say: "Family Killed by Snake They Did Not Know."

All this went through my mind while I frantically phoned my dear neighbors Nelle and Jim to report, at the top of my lungs, "I have a snake!"

Jim came right over with a rake, entangled the snake in the rake, and pitched the raked snake into the woods. Done.

From her perch in my bedroom, Cosmo could observe all the excitement over the snake, though she couldn't quite see the snake. What she could see was Jim's rake. She growled menacingly at it. Maybe she thought it was a snake, a straight,

stiff snake. In Africa, snakes are natural predators of African grey nestlings and fledglings.

Jim said that the snake, about four feet long, was probably a rat snake, common to the southeast and harmless to humans. In other words, it was a "good snake." But when I googled Rat snakes, I learned that they eat rats, mice, squirrels, birds, and bird eggs. From Cosmo's perspective, my snake was not a good snake.

Anyway, this event made me realize how inseparable our human habitats are from the natural habitats we take over. I don't know much about snakes, so I am afraid of them. And Western literature, beginning with Genesis, has turned the snake into a symbol of evil. But I chose to live in snake territory. The snakes were here before commercial developers bought this part of Clarke County, called it a neighborhood, laid out streets and lots, built houses, and turned the woods over to house dwellers to control or to *try* to control.

Even the most adamant civilization-loving humans cannot fully control the rest of nature. Snakes will slither their way into our gardens, onto our decks, and into our homes unless we completely destroy their habitat. So do we pave paradise and put up a parking lot?

But we really don't want to destroy the snakes' habitat. Snakes, like all other animals, have a job to do wherever they live. If we accidentally wipe them out, we change the lifestyles, dining habits, and reproductive success of everybody else in their habitat. For example, if the rat snake disappears from the woods, the rats will multiply, and more rats will scurry their way into our gardens, onto our decks, and into our homes.

In nature, there are neither good species nor bad species. There are just different species, all dependent in one way or another on each other. If we pollute the water, air, and soil, change the planet's climate, and destroy the habitats of our fellow residents of Earth we're threatening everybody's future.

We're not smart enough to predict all the changes that will take place in even one ecosystem if one or more species disappear. In accidentally decreasing the whole planet's biodiversity, we may unintentionally damage our own lifestyles, dining habits, and reproductive success. Most of us would not like that.

CHAPTER 50

Modifying One's Environment

MY SPONGE BILL IS WAY HIGH.

One summer evening some friends came by to see Cosmo and have a glass of wine. I think they also wanted to see me too, although I'm not sure. Cosmo is much more interesting to human folks than I am.

Cosmo talks, but she also walks. While we humans were enjoying our wine and cheese, Cosmo climbed down from her cage, walked into the kitchen, opened the cabinet door under the sink, pulled out a new package of blue sponges, ripped the cellophane, extracted a sponge, and proceeded to destroy it.

Just about the time I noticed her absence from the living room, I heard Cosmo say to herself, very softly, "No, no."

I rushed into the kitchen to find pieces of blue sponge all over the kitchen floor. Cosmo dropped the remnant of the sponge, looked up at me, and said, "Hi!"

This was not the first time Cosmo had gone under the sink to get a sponge, nor was it the last. She remembers where I keep new sponges, and she goes after them every chance she gets.

If I had to state Cosmo's mission in life, I'd say it's to modify her environment. Wherever she goes in the house, Cosmo changes what was already there. If she's on the kitchen counter, she picks up forks and drops them on the floor. If she's on the kitchen floor, she hauls pots and pans out of the cupboard. If she's on her car cage, she removes the fasteners of the food dishes and dumps their contents onto the table. If she's in my bathroom she pulls open the cosmetic drawers, extracts their content, and scatters emery boards, dental floss, lipsticks, eyeliners, and blush across the room.

If she's in my study, she pulls the books off the shelves. If she finds a pen, she takes it apart. If she gets access to a base-board, she turns it into sawdust. If she gets access to toes, she bites them. If I go outside, she mimics the ring of the phone, and I run in to get it. I could go on.

When I catch her doing something forbidden she says "Uh, oh."

In exasperation, I've wondered why in creation Cosmo won't leave things where they are. But then I've thought: What do I want her to do? Stand still on top of a cage—or worse, incarcerated in a cage—look pretty, talk and whistle all day long? Of course I don't.

Asking Cosmo to stand still would be like asking kudzu to grow nicely in a flower bed.

Come to think of it, Cosmo is an exotic invasive species in my household. I invited her in, so I should expect the chaos she brings.

Everybody modifies his or her environment in the course of doing what comes naturally. That includes people, parrots, platypuses, pandas, panthers, possums, pumas, peacocks, pi-ranhas, petunias, plankton. Beavers and gophers, who are eco-system engineers, do it big-time. So does kudzu, known by Southerners as "the plant that ate the South."

Wild animals in their natural habitat follow their urges to eat, fend off competitors, make babies, and have a little fun along the way. They hunt, fish, or graze, making small changes to their environment with every bite they take. The woods are never the same from day to day, year to year. Nor is the desert. Nor the tundra. Nor the seas, lakes, rivers, and streams.

We've known this since the ancient Greek philosopher Heraclitus observed, "Everything changes and nothing re-mains still" "You cannot step twice into the same stream."

We don't much notice how wild animals, with the possible exception of beavers and gophers, modify their environments. If they are living where their ancestors lived, most of them don't change their habitat irreversibly.

A newcomer whose ancestors lived elsewhere does change

the habitat because the newcomer without natural predators in his adopted environment may proliferate uncontrollably and outcompete the old-timers for food. That's what kudzu, armadillos, and fire ants are doing in Georgia.

I don't want to contemplate the question of whether humans act like invasive, non-native species in our planetary ecosystem. Not now.

Anyway, I wanted Cosmo to invade my world, and I've accepted happily the fundamental changes she's wrought in my habitat. In fact, I've come to admire my dear parrot's heroic efforts to have an exciting, fun-filled, intellectually stimulating life in a foreign land—my house—where no parrot has walked before.

I understand that not everybody will love a parrot. Some folks will prefer kudzu.

CHAPTER 51

Altruism

YESTERDAY IN THE KITCHEN I let Cosmo sample just about everything I was preparing: cucumber, peas, red bell pepper, and pine nuts. We had our usual fun eating together, talking, whistling, and listening to music while I cooked.

After a while Cosmo asked, "Do you wanna dance?" With the volume up on the stereo, we danced to "*Azul,*" sung by Mexican singer Cristián Castro.

We danced. That is, Cosmo clung tightly to my left hand while I swung her high and low to the beat of "*Fue una mañana que yo te encontré .*"

Cosmo asked for a kiss. I was wary. I'd seen that look in her eyes before. She was jerking her head back and forth. Suddenly she had a perfectly intact green pea in her beak. She tried to place it in my mouth.

When I declined her offering, Cosmo ground up the pea, swallowed it, and like magic produced another one. And another. She had stored the peas in her crop. I put her back on her perch.

Some parrot behaviorists say that Cosmo is treating me as her mate and will warn me not to encourage her to regurgitate food for me. I promise not to encourage her to regurgitate food for me. Maggie Wright, author of an African grey owner's manual, will advise me to accept the offering in my hand and tell Cosmo "Thank you." That's what I'll do next time.

African greys are social eaters. In the rain forest they share food and eat together in their large flock. Cosmo expects the same in her home with her small flock. Whenever I have company, Cosmo looks at the spread on the dinner table and says, "Cosmo wanna corn!"

Since she doesn't have a big food vocabulary Cosmo says "corn" to signify whatever food she wants. She's distressed if I deny her a morsel. For her, my dinnertime is her dinnertime, or ought to be.

Humans are social eaters too. We have shared food with each other since we lived in caves. We exchange ideas and build friendships over meals. We honor each other and commemorate our unity with feasts. Sharing food is an altruistic act in the short term and is an act that brings the sharer the reward of enduring relationships in the long term.

Non-human primates share food with each other both in the jungle and in the lab. Researchers tested the generosity of chimpanzees and Capuchin monkeys at Emory's Yerkes Research Center. They found that when the primates are given the choice of either food for themselves alone or food for themselves and a friend they request food for two. The generous primate expects the friend to reciprocate. The two thereby form a relationship.

Vampire bats, who must eat at least every seventy hours, will regurgitate a bit of blood for a hungry, weak bat who has gone a night or two without successful hunting. Scientists at the University of Maryland observed that bats offer food not just to their relatives but also to other bats who have previously given food to them. They reciprocate. Unselfish bats survive, and their colony thrives. Good deal.

Evolutionary biologist Robert Trivers coined the term "reciprocal altruism" for the subordination of an animal's immediate needs to the needs of another in the expectation that the other will return the favor later. I'll bet we can find lots of examples of it throughout the animal kingdom.

In human society we know reciprocal altruism as unselfishness. It's the basis of friendship, partnership, loyalty, love.

Cosmo's attempt to give me food that she'd stored in her craw is an act motivated by her instinct to strengthen the bond between us. Cosmo is driven by natural desires in an unnatural environment. Nature urges her to feed the one she loves, who would normally be another African Grey parrot. But she lives with two dogs and a human. So she adapts. She feeds the one she's with, me. I am featherless, but available.

What lesson can we draw from Cosmo's reciprocal altruism, or unselfishness, or whatever we call her act of regurgitation of the peas she had once intended to keep for herself? Perhaps it is that we can learn to love somebody very different from ourselves, somebody who may not be our size or our kind of animal. That we can build ties to groups that are unlike us. That we can learn to live together, love each other, and become unselfish.

Dining together reduces animosities. So let's make dinner not war.

CHAPTER 52

Vocal Learning

ONE LATE NIGHT ABOUT A WEEK AGO when I thought I'd finally persuaded her to hop on my hand, Cosmo flipped over
backwards on her perch, looked at me upside down, and said,
"There you are!" She chuckled. It was her bedtime, and she
didn't feel a bit sleepy.

Now Cosmo and I have a new bedtime routine, not of my
choosing. I try to get Cosmo to step onto my hand, and she
does everything she can to frustrate me. She flops backwards
or forwards on her perch. She hangs upside down by one foot.
She goes limp like a protester.

Between tricks she returns to her perch and taunts me.
"Betty Jean wanna come here?" I approach her, and she says
"Noooooooooooo" and laughs uproariously.

"Cosmo wanna kiss!" I put my head up hopefully, and she
says, "Noooooooooooo" and leans away with a chuckle.

Cosmo and I are playmates. We play games with each
other. In order to play we must anticipate what the other one
is expecting.

Does that mean that individuals of different species, as different as humans and birds, who play with each other have
similar thought patterns? Could humans and birds have similar brains?

Duke University neurobiologist Erich Jarvis, who studies
hummingbird and songbird brains, says that to some extent
we do. Jarvis and his colleagues have examined the brain—
clusters of neurons in the brain that enable vocal learning in
songbirds, hummingbirds, and parrots, and they have found
similarities with comparable parts of the human brain.

In an article in *Science Daily*, Jarvis elaborates.

> While all birds vocalize, for most of them these
> sounds are genetically hardwired. Only songbirds,
> parrots and hummingbirds have the ability to learn
> songs. This type of vocal learning is similar to the way
> that humans learn to speak.

Amazing. Go to Erich Jarvis's website to see side-by-side pictures of the bird brain and the human brain.

In another article in *Science Daily*, Duke neurobiologist Richard Mooney explains the evolutionary advantage of this brain development in songbirds. "Many skills, including communication skills, require great precision if you want to stay in the gene pool. A male songbird has to learn to sing precisely or he won't attract a mate."

Vocal learning is the form of intelligence that makes complex language possible in humans and simpler language possible in parrots, hummingbirds, and songbirds as well as in dolphins and whales. Of course, vocal learners also have the physical capacity for sound production. Vocal learners, who acquire their vocalizations from their parents and their flock or pod mates before sexual maturity can use hundreds of different calls to communicate with each other.

I can attest to the long learning period for parrots. Cosmo learned to talk over a period of four or five years until she reached sexual maturity. After that, she picked up fewer words, although she continued to use her big vocabulary of more than a hundred and sixty-five words, as well as the Cosmo-grammar that I had taught her, to make new and sometimes unusual sentences.

Why are we astounded that parrots, hummingbirds, and songbirds are highly intelligent vocal learners with brain structures not totally dissimilar from our own, and not astounded that dolphins and whales are highly intelligent vocal learners?

I'd say that from time immemorial humans have ranked mammals higher on the smartness scale than birds simply because we're mammals. We know we're smart. We've assumed that birds were driven mainly by instinct and were therefore less smart. We've just have not understood birds.

This brings me back to my independent-minded, joke-telling, back-talking, fun-loving parrot. If Cosmo's brain is like mine, even a little like mine, in physical capacity for vocal learning, I should not be surprised that she and I play together, tease each other, and predict each other's responses to our actions. She is predisposed brain-wise to learn her whistles and her words from me, to combine them into new melodies and utterances, and to pay attention to what I am doing and saying.

This morning, as I write, Cosmo is answering a cardinal outside in the woods. The cardinal is calling, "Purdy purdy purdy." Cosmo is calling back, "Purdy purdy purdy." The outdoor cardinal is calling his mate, as he is genetically hardwired to do. Cosmo is playing.

CHAPTER 53

Prejudices

"**W**HERE'S COSMO?"

That's Cosmo calling. I'm supposed to go find her. It's a game we play. This morning I'll keep writing. Pretty soon she'll come back to find me.

I thought about how much I love her and how much I like all birds. Even though I know they can bite, I'm not afraid of birds, not crows, not hawks, not even ostriches, not the way I'm afraid of snakes.

But I've learned that not all humans like birds. Some folks my age saw Alfred Hitchcock's 1963 movie *The Birds* in their formative period, and they've never recovered.

Are they prejudiced against birds? Am I prejudiced against snakes? Are readers of "Little Red Riding Hood" prejudiced against wolves?

I suspect our prejudices have led to our mistreatment of other animals and our underestimation of their intelligence. It's impossible to look at the world without prejudices of some kind or other.

Think of our language. When we're being uncomplimetary, we call people bird-brain, or catty, or jack-ass," or snake, or chicken, or, worst of all, rat. What did these animals do to deserve comparison with individuals we want to insult?

We call irresponsible people "flighty," unintentionally insulting the avian community. We also say "gypped," insulting the Gypsies, "go Dutch," insulting the Hollanders, and a host of other words and phrases that emerged out of our ancestors' prejudices against people different from themselves.

Remember all the parrot jokes, which depict parrots as mindless repeaters of what they've overheard and not as "man's best friend."

Fairy tales, movies, novels, textbooks, newspapers, sermons—all that our culture teaches us—make us think one way or another about birds, snakes, wolves, other humans, everything under the sun. We inherit prejudices embedded in our culture. Unwittingly, we pass them on to future generations.

I spent my career as a teacher, so I believe in book-learning. But I recognize that the best way to overcome prejudices against certain species, races, ethnicities, and religions is to get to know individuals in the flesh. Children who have rats for pets don't hate them. Children who play with snakes, nonpoisonous ones, don't fear them. Children who like birds don't call anybody bird-brained.

People young and old who have neighbors of different skin color, place of origin, or religion, learn that likability is not confined to likeness.

My friends, Valerie and Bob, recently acquired chickens, whom they named Rosie, Emily, Edie, Penny Louise, and Buffy Marie. Buffy Marie is the leader of the flock, Rosie is aggressive, and Emily, Edie, and Penny Louise are very affectionate to each other and to their human caregivers. The chickens look alike to folks who don't know them, but to Valerie and Bob the chickens are unmistakably different from each other. They each have their own distinctive, delightful personalities. To Valerie and Bob, who love them, they are not cowardly. Neither are they "poultry."

CHAPTER 54

Noise and Reproduction

COSMO LOVES TO ENTERTAIN ME from near and far.

Yesterday morning, Cosmo left my study and waddled down the hall to her roost cage for a snack. I noticed that on her way she'd deposited a tiny bit of poop on the floor. I got up, retrieved the Windex and a paper towel, sprayed the spot, and . . .

Instantly, Cosmo called loudly, very loudly, from her room, "That's spray for Cosmo poop!" She made sure I heard her. Then she chuckled.

I don't know whether Cosmo chuckles at appropriate times because she finds the situation funny or because she thinks that I will find the situation funny. At any rate, she sounds like me and not an African grey in the Congo.

Cosmo enjoys life.

This afternoon I'm back at my computer, and Cosmo is perched atop her cage in my bedroom. She's mimicking me actually, she's mocking me.

She's saying in my voice: "Oh, no. What's that? No, no, no! Bad bird! Don't bite! No, no, no, no, no, no, no, no! Cosmo go back in cage! Cosmo is a bad bird." Then she laughs.. Apparently, she finds my scoldings funny. She seems to be re-membering them with pleasure.

Now she is yelling, "I'm here! Betty Jean, come here!"

I've noticed that Cosmo adjusts the pitch of her voice to the need for me to hear her. If she's with me, she speaks softly. If she's far away, she speaks loudly.

I read online that some city birds sing at higher frequencies than their country brothers. At Leiden University in the Netherlands, behavior ecologist Wouter Halfwerk, studied a bird called the great tit, a larger European cousin of our titmouse.

Halfwerk noticed that the males sing high-pitched tunes when in a noisy environment to make themselves heard by the females. The problem is that the females don't like the high-frequency songs as much as they like the lower, sexier songs of the males who don't have to raise their voices. In an article published in the *Proceedings of the National Academy of Sciences*, Halfwerk reported that great tit females were more likely to cheat on males with high-frequency songs than on males with low-frequency songs. The scientists proved this by paternity tests on the eggs. Oh, my.

Halfwerk wrote: "If females can hear all song types equally well, they will go for the sexy ones, but if they cannot hear the sexy ones well anymore, then they might just go for the songs they can still hear."

Other researchers have discovered that female great tits who mate with songsters of the upper registers lay fewer eggs.

This is evidence that noise pollution interferes with reproduction.

Some birds who are not vocal learners, such as doves, are not capable of changing their song. They go unheard in noisy areas. That's not good for reproduction either.

By the way, the word "noise," from the early thirteenth century, is related etymologically to the word nausea, which in Latin means "disgust, annoyance, discomfort," and literally "seasickness."

I wonder: Are we making ourselves sick with noise pollution? We know that loud, continuous noise causes hearing impairment and tinnitus as well as irritability and anxiety in humans. What does it do to the birds and the bees? Firecrackers and gunshots frighten me and scare birds off their perches. Do firecrackers and gunshots cause post-traumatic stress in other animals?

For years the National Audubon Society has been reporting declines in the populations of many common North

American birds. Meadowlarks and grassland birds are disappearing because of suburban sprawl, intensified farming, and industrial development. The boreal chickadee and other forest-dwelling birds are losing their natural habitats because of logging, mining, and drilling. Who knows what birds vacated their homeland when we built our cities.

Humans know well that the destruction of the homes of our fellow residents of Earth affects their survival. But in trying to preserve the habitats of birds, bears, whales, frogs, and fish, we may have thought more about their physical environment than their auditory environment. We knew we were inflicting harm when we chopped down their trees and poured waste into their rivers and streams, but we didn't know we were inflicting harm when we flew our noisy jets over their woods, steered our noisy ships through their oceans, and lived our noisy lives wherever we went.

Now we know that environmental noise makes birds sing higher and louder, like humans. In a crowded restaurant, humans talk higher and louder. Everybody shouts and nobody hears. Soon the world may resemble a crowded restaurant.

When my dog Mary goes out on the deck and starts barking, Cosmo screams, "Mary, come here!" at the top of her lungs. Kaylee barks to express her annoyance with Mary and Cosmo. Then I holler, "Doggies, don't bark!" Cosmo joins in. "Woo woo woo." Mary barks louder.

CHAPTER 55

Avian Dinosaurs

COSMO BRINGS INTO OUR HOME the calls, songs, chatter, and conversations of all our woodsy neighbors. One morning she mimicked crows, cardinals, blue jays, finches, wrens, titmice and a host of other birds who feed on our deck railing, Oh, yes, and squirrels.

If my eyes had been closed I'd have sworn I was sitting down by the creek.

Cosmo then walked into my study, announced "Here I am!" and climbed to the top of the cage behind me. To please her I went to the Cornell Lab of Ornithology website and played her a few songs of other Georgia birds.

I did not play her any hawk calls, however. Once I played too loudly a recording of a red-shouldered hawk when Cosmo was in the other room. Cosmo abruptly flew off her perch. Although from the safety of her roost cage Cosmo often mimics the hawk's call, which she hears out in the woods, she must have been startled to hear the loud call inside our house. The hawk is a predator of parrots, and Cosmo recognized the danger instinctively.

Did parrots develop their mimicry to deceive their predators? A hawk might not attack a parrot who spoke like a hawk. I certainly wouldn't stomp on a cockroach who spoke like a human.

I read that female mocking birds are attracted most to the males with the largest repertoire of songs. One male mocker was observed to mimic fifty-five different species in one hour. The female mocking birds recognized the male mocker's voice anyway. I'll bet a lot of them wanted to mate with him for his sweet music. And then they would pass on his mimicry genes to their offspring.

On the web I come across little information on the evolution of parrots and the evolutionary advantage their mimicry of sound gave them, but there is much information on the evolution of birds in general.

Scientists generally agree that birds appeared during the Mesozoic Era, which extended from two hundred fifty to sixty-five million years ago. They evolved from the small dinosaurs that possessed feathers and a beak. Only the small avian dinosaurs survived the mass extinction event of sixty-five million years ago when their larger relatives died in the sudden change of climate probably caused by a giant asteroid hitting the planet.

A paleontology graduate student, Ryan McKellar, discovered feathers in an eighty-million-year-old piece of amber. The tiny feathers were of two types: dinosaur-ish feathers and bird-ish feathers. Amber, which is fossilized tree resin, has preserved insects, spiders, leaves, and feathers from as long ago as one hundred thirty-five million years, and it has been prized as jewelry by humans for the past thirteen thousand years.

Paleontologist Amanda Falk of the University of Kansas, working in South Korea, found fossilized tracks of shore birds from one hundred ten million years ago very similar to the tracks of herons. She and her colleagues have deduced that these ancient birds must have been wader fishermen—or wader fisher birds—not altogether different from today's wader birds.

Researchers unearthed the fossilized bones of parrots who inhabited the humid forests of Europe twenty million years ago.

Scientists have accumulated much evidence to show physical connections in bone structures between avian dinosaurs and our modern-day birds. And they have discovered that the lungs of theropod dinosaurs—carnivorous dinosaurs that walked on two legs and had birdlike feet—resemble birds' lungs.

Yet nobody has shown conclusively how the avian dinosaurs came to fly.

When I think of the evolutionary roots of Cosmo, the hawks, the crows, and all Earth's other living creatures, I ponder with awe the short time humans have populated our planet. Anatomically modern Homo sapiens—our kind of human—have been around for perhaps only two hundred thousand years, way short of a million. Birds flew a long time before we walked.

When I write in the evenings, Cosmo often asks for kisses. Tonight she said, "Betty Jean kiss feathers, okay?"

"Okay, Cosmo. Betty Jean kiss feathers," I responded. I kissed them.

"We're gonna go to cuddle?" Her grammar was not perfect, but her message was clear.

She stepped onto my left hand, gripped it tightly with her dinosaur-ish toes, and flipped herself over backwards into my lap. Then she closed her eyes in anticipation of my caresses.

Cosmo's feathers are beautiful. Mostly shades of gray, except for the delicate white facial feathers and the glorious red tail feathers.

When did parrots get their brilliant colors? I wondered. The dinosaur-ish feathers in the amber were brown.

CHAPTER 56

Friends

I CONSIDER COSMO, MARY, AND KAYLEE to be family. We act like a family, but we're more accurately dear friends since we're not closely related to each other genetically. Cosmo has feathers, Mary and Kaylee have fur, and I have, well, clothes—

I looked up the word friend in the Oxford English Dictionary. According to the OED, a friend is "a person joined by affection and intimacy to another, independently of sexual or family love." And a person is "an individual human being; specifically a human being as opposed to a thing or an animal."

According to the *Free Online Dictionary*, a friend is "a person whom one knows, likes, and trusts," and a person is "a living human."

Whoa. These anthropocentric definitions are way out of date. They must have been written before humans officially recognized in the 2012 Cambridge Declaration on Consciousness that all mammals and birds, as well as octopuses have a brain that can support consciousness. It seems obvious that if an animal has thoughts and feelings, he can have friends.

I would define friend as "an animal, human or non-human, joined to another by affection, intimacy, trust, and empathy, independently of sexual or family love." I add empathy, because I think a friend must be able to feel your pain.

My brother Branch sent me a video of an orangutan and a Bluetick coon hound seeing each other and bonding immediately. Their eyes met, their faces lit up, they raced to each other. Surya the orangutan embraced Roscoe the dog with his seven-foot arm span. They've stayed together. Surya hugs Roscoe, shares food with him, walks him on a leash, and swims with him. Roscoe rewards Surya with devotion. I'd say they are best friends.

Eliot Zapata sent me a video of a female Leopard seal in the Antarctic making her acquaintance with National Geographic photographer Paul Nicklen. For four days the seal supplied Paul with penguins including strong penguins, weak penguins, dead penguins, and penguin nuggets. The seal tried to feed Paul despite Paul's perplexing lack of appetite. That's kindness.

If Surya had encountered a pack of dogs he probably would have fled. If Roscoe had encountered a buffoonery of orangutans, he for sure would have fled. If the seal had encountered an army of men, the seal would not have brought one of them a penguin.

How would you feel if you met a harem of seals, a mob of kangaroos, a gaggle of geese, a conspiracy of ravens, a company of parrots, or a horde of humans who were strangers to you? You might judge them by their teeth, their talons, their beaks, their horns, their garments, their guns. You'd not let them get close. You'd feel safer if they were gone, out of sight, off the radar screen, rendered harmless.

But if all by yourself, you met a big, gentle kangaroo who was all by herself, wouldn't you hold out your hand to her? You might give her a name: Pouchpotato. You'd want to see Pouchpotato again.

If you met a lone raven, you might feed him and give him a name: Lone Raven. After you and Lone Raven had spent time together and learned to trust each other, you might want to touch his feathers, and he might let you.

It seems like friendship requires one-on-one, face-to-face, look-into-each-other's-eyes, see-into-each-other's-soul interaction. Enmity does not.

I've always marveled at how animals learn each other's thoughts and feelings by looking into each other's eyes. We must believe that's where the soul resides.

But we have to get close to look into each other's eyes. And if we get close we might become friends.

Chapter 57

Ethical Community

ONE DAY I WATCHED MY LITTLE DOG Mary lean over the edge of the bed as far as she could without falling off. She was dangling an old rag of a toy, which had once been a stuffed monkey, just above Cosmo's head. She wanted Cosmo to grab it. Cosmo was trying her best to grab it, but she wasn't tall enough. The toy fell on the floor.

Another day, when I was preparing to take my dogs for a walk, I watched Mary and Cosmo play "go for a walk." I had already leashed up Mary, who was jumping up and down in anticipation of going outside. While I was leashing up Kaylee, Cosmo grabbed the end of Mary's leash in her beak. Mary immediately stopped jumping and led Cosmo slowly down the hall. Mary was allowing Cosmo the pleasure of taking her for a walk. They proceeded for about five feet before Cosmo dropped the leash.

Cosmo and Mary are friends. In my household Cosmo the sixteen-ounce parrot, Mary the twelve-pound dog, Kaylee the twenty-pound dog, and I the heavier human are all friends. Actually, we are family. Mary and Kaylee could easily eat Cosmo if they wanted, but they don't. Cosmo could easily attack them, but she doesn't. And all of them could gang up on me, but they don't. The four of us have formed an ethical community, like mixed households everywhere. We trust each other and we cooperate with each other for the happiness and well-being of all.

When guests come to the door, Mary, Kaylee, and Cosmo welcome them as I do, because they trust me. They cooperate with the guests rather than treat them as prey.

My favorite essay about cooperation is "The Land Ethic,"

written by Aldo Leopold in the 1940s.

Leopold said that when humans who are different from each other realize we are dependent on each other, we cooperate. We once cooperated only with people who looked like us, spoke our language, and shared our values. That was our ethical community then, our tribe. We believed we did not need to be nice to those outside it.

Gradually, we realized that cooperation, such as commerce, with fellow humans from diverse groups would benefit everybody. We expanded our ethical community to include those other humans. Eventually, we expanded our ethical community to include all humans in the world. The concept of universal human rights exemplifies this. The Universal Declaration of Human Rights, proposed by Eleanor Roosevelt as chair of the UN Commission on Human Rights, was adopted by the United Nations General Assembly in December of 1948.

Leopold argued that when humans come to realizethat we are dependent on "the land," by which he meant the entire ecosystem, we will include our natural environment in our ethical community.

Many years later we see how right Leopold was. We now have legislation—not enough, in my opinion, but some—as well as protecting endangered ecosystems and endangered species, prohibiting cruelty to animals. With our increasing awareness of the relationship between human activity and global climate change, throughout the world we are passing legislation to protect the planet from ourselves.

I think about Leopold's essay when I watch animals of different species play together. When an individual, human or non-human, forms a friendship with a very different kind of individual, he or she must be able to recognize a "personality"a soul, or a self in the other individual.

Those of us who have dogs, cats, birds, and horses as friends already understand this. We certainly see our pets as having personalities. When we name them, we bring them into our ethical community. When we refer to them, we use the pronoun who not it."

We tend not to name the squirrels, possums, raccoons, skunks, armadillos, deer, hawks, crows, blue jays, finches, frogs, and fish who live outside our homes. When we don't name them, we may be disinclined to treat them as part of our ethical community.

Yet animals have personalities too and thoughts and feelings, and probably the capacity for friendship within their species and beyond.

By the way, although I eat mostly seafood and fish, I occasionally eat meat. I feel bad about this, especially when I follow a chicken truck down the highway. I do hope that we can find ways to improve the lives of the animals we raise for our consumption. We don't have to name them to include them in our extended ethical community. Cows, sheep, pigs, and chickens have personalities, whether we know them up close and personal or not.

I recognize that not all human and non-human animals on Earth can be friends with each other. We all get hungry. May our inteentions be ethical nontheless.

CHAPTER 58

Senses

"RRRING RRRING RRRING. You have reached 5496243. Thank you. Good-bye. Beep!"

Cosmo mimics the answering machine. She knows my phone number, but she has no idea what the number means, or even that it's a number.

After the number, she'll often utter in a very low, guttural voice some nonsensical syllables that sound like English if you are French. After the beep, she'll laugh.

When my phone actually rang the other day, Cosmo called out, "Telephone for Betty Jean!" She knows that means: that I rush to the phone, pick it up, and start talking to no one, not to the dogs, not to her.

I answered the phone and, after a bit of conversation, asked my friend to say Hello to Cosmo.

I held the phone to Cosmo's ear. Birds do have ears, just not the stick-out, floppy kind. Cosmo listened intently and then in a low, almost inaudible voice said, "Hello." Nothing else.

I've come to the realization that Cosmo does not associate the sounds she hears in the phone with voices of live people. She hasn't been taught that voices can travel over wires and radio waves.

So much of what humans hear and see in the world is related to what we've been taught. We've been taught how things are connected to each other and what causes what. We've been taught who are the good guys and who are the bad. We've been taught which are the tasty animals, such as shrimp, and which are the nasty ones, such as roaches.

We approach what we see in language. Our words divide up the world into categories, position us in our environment, and define our relationships to each other and to everything else.

We explain to each other the way we think the world works, and then we see and hear the world according to how we think about it. As poet Wallace Stevens wrote in "A Postcard from the Volcano" we pass on to future generations "the look of things" and "what we felt at what we saw."

We are often wrong. We used to think the Earth was the center of the universe.

Living with Cosmo has taught me many lessons. One of them is that no matter how hard humans try to observe nature objectively, we really can't. We're stuck with our ideas, which influence how we perceive things. We're also limited by our senses.

I can't see the world the way Cosmo sees it, not even if I look up from six inches off the ground. She sees things better than I do, and in much greater detail.

Like other daytime birds, Cosmo sees into the ultraviolet spectrum of light whereas owls and other nighttime birds see into the infrared spectrum.

Mantis shrimp, who have extraordinarily complex eyes, see into both ultraviolet and infrared light ranges. I wonder what the deep sea looks like to them.

Most birds also hear better than humans. They hear in greater detail. For example, when we humans hear one long note, birds hear separate notes. Birds can distinguish fine nuances in a note that we cannot, and that's how they recognize the call of their mate.

Owls, who have large ear holes and extremely keen hearing, hear sounds that we humans don't hear at all. So do elephants and jaguars. Elephants can hear at extremely low frequencies, and jaguars at very high frequencies.

Bears and dogs have an exceptionally keen sense of smell.

Different animals experience the world differently.

Furthermore, everybody on the planet notices different things, because we all have different interests and values.

When I walk in the woods, I look for deer. When my dogs Kaylee and Mary walk in the woods, they look for deer poop, to rub on their necks. When my former student Buck Trible walks in the woods, he looks for ants. Armadillos look for ants, too.

I get dizzy thinking about all the different worlds the trillions of Earth's non-human animals experience. And all the different worlds the billions of Earth's human animals experience. None is quite like mine.

How in the world can we ever get along? How can we communicate?

Yet we do.

CHAPTER 59

Historical Parrots

THE OTHER DAY I HEARD A CRASH in the bathroom, followed by Cosmo's comment to herself: "Oh no bad bird no no no."

"Oh, no!" I exclaimed. "Cosmo, where are you?"

I found her on top of the counter in my guest bathroom awaiting my arrival. She'd opened the door to the cabinet below, climbed onto the plastic wastebasket, and knocked over the wastebasket while seizing hold of the counter's edge.

"Cosmo!"

"Cosmooo-oo-oo!" she echoed, not as respectfully as I might have desired.

I put her on the floor and started picking up the wastebasket's scattered contents. Cosmo scurried across the hall into my bedroom as fast as she could, extending her wings to gain speed, and hurriedly ascended to the rope perch out of my reach. She didn't want to be incarcerated for her misdeed.

Why would anybody with any semblance of reason keep a parrot? I wondered.

Yet through the centuries, many fairly normal people, even important people, have kept parrots.

Aristotle kept a "human tongued" parrot he called Psittace. Psittace is the origin of the scientific name for the parrot family, Psittacine.

The Holy Roman Emperor Frederick II kept an umbrella cockatoo.

Queen Isabella owned a pair of Amazons that Christopher Columbus picked up for her in Cuba. They must have had a rough voyage to Spain.

In the sixteenth, seventeenth, and eighteenth centuries, when European explorers were returning to Europe with colorful parrots they'd encountered in Africa and the New World, caged birds became fashionable among the aristocracy. Parrots brought amusement and beauty into a parlor. Canaries brought music.

King Henry VIII owned an African Grey. So did Marie Antoinette, whose grey must have spoken French. Queen Victoria had a grey named Coco who could sing "God Save the rQueen." King George V had a roseate cockatoo named Charlotte, who accompanied him on his travels.

A half-dozen American presidents lived with parrots.

First Lady Martha Washington had a parrot named Polly who didn't get along with her husband George. First Lady Dolley Madison had a military macaw who perched on her shoulder at official White House receptions. President Andrew Jackson had a parrot named Pol who cussed at his funeral and had to be escorted out.

President William McKinley had a double yellow-headed Amazon named Washington Post who could sing "Yankee Doodle." President Teddy Roosevelt had a hyacinth macaw named Eli Yale. President John Kennedy had parakeets named Bluebelle and Marybelle.

I wonder about the lives of these parrots. What happened to Marie Antoinette's parrot when the queen lost her head? Did Dolley's parrot poop on her evening gown? What did Pol say that got him removed from his master's funeral? How nice that Andrew invited Pol to his funeral.

Anyway, Cosmo is in good company. Were these First Birds loved as much as my dear Cosmo? I imagine so. They probably all had fancy cages, appropriate to the architectural style of the era but probably much smaller than parrots need. I hope that these parrots enjoyed freedom out of their cages.

President Calvin Coolidge and First Lady Grace had canaries. They called them Nick and Tuck. They also had raccoons, Rebecca and Horace; lion cubs, Tax Reduction and Budget Bureau; a donkey, Ebeneezer; a goose, Enoch; a bobcat, Smoky; a pygmy hippo, Billy; a cat, Tiger; a wallaby; an antelope; a black bear; and eleven dogs. I guess the press referred to Enoch as First Goose.

I love finding out the names that people give their pets. To name an animal is to give him or her the respect that every animal, in my opinion, deserves. What must go through an animal's mind—or an infant human's mind, for that matter—when she discovers she has a name?

I did not change Cosmo's name when the vet told me that my bird was a female, because Cosmo had already learned her name. She already knew that when I called "Cosmo" I was calling her. She had already figured out that she, Cosmo, was a bird and that Blanche was a dog.

When Cosmo hears her name, Cosmo must think, "That's me!"

CHAPTER 60

Pets

EVERY MORNING WHEN I GET UP I see my faithful little mother squirrel watching me move through the house from the deck railing where she awaits her breakfast. She knows my habits and I know hers. We are well acquainted with each other. We like each other.

I put out bird seed and deer corn for her and her fellow squirrels, chipmunks, and birds, who all dine here.

Then I go back inside to fix breakfast for Cosmo, Kaylee, Mary, and me.

Today, after we'd eaten, Cosmo scurried over to the sliding glass door and summoned me: "Look, that's birdie!"

Cosmo had seen three gorgeous crows land on the railing to join the squirrels for breakfast. She called out to them, "Caw, caw!"

Mary heard Cosmo and raced out the doggie door to make the crows flap their wings and fly onto the roof. Mary takes great pleasure in causing a flurry of feathers.

Kaylee heard Mary and barked.

Then I went into the bathroom to put on my make-up. Suddenly I heard a commotion behind me. Cosmo was on the floor yanking the comforter, and Mary was on the bed indignantly trying to get Cosmo to release it.

I turned around, ready to stop the action. Cosmo looked up at me, dropped the comforter, and said, "Hi."

I live in a zoo, I thought in exasperation.

But no, not really. Residents of a zoo live in confinement and interact mainly with their zookeeper. They are under the zookeeper's control.

I live in a village whose residents happen to be of different species, some of them making their life indoors, some of them making their life outdoors. They interact with each other and don't obey me. These animals aren't under anybody's control. They still have a tiny bit of wildness in them—well, more than a tiny bit in Cosmo's case.

I like them that way. I want them all to feel free to be their true animal self.

We humans love our animals, be they feathery, furry, hairy, or scaly, be they indoor or outdoor. And we want them to love us.

What's interesting is that humans all over the world keep animals as pets, and have done so for millennia. Paleontologists have unearthed evidence for the domestication of dogs some fifteen thousand years ago and the domestication of cats some nine thousand years ago.

Archaeologists have discovered pictures of dogs resembling today's sight hounds in Egyptian tombs of three thousand BCE, and a cat with a collar in an Egyptian tomb of twenty-four hundred BCE. In Egyptian hieroglyphics, they've found depictions of caged doves and parrots.

Of course, Egypt is not the only ancient culture that kept pets. But Egyptians left good records.

I wonder whether the keeping of pets is related to our coming in out of the wild and getting civilized when we became indoor people. Maybe we civilized humans don't want a complete separation from the wild.

I read that thirty-nine percent of American households include at least one dog, thirty-three percent at least one cat, twelve percent at least one fish, four-point-six percent at least one bird, and thirty-five percent at least one plant.

Nearly seventeen percent of us feed wild birds. Probably the same seventeen percent feed wild squirrels, though perhaps unintentionally. I couldn't find statistics for squirrel feeding.

Humans have come a long way from the time we lived in the wilderness and huddled together around a fire in fear of wolves, bears, and mountain lions, whose scary eyes we thought we saw gleaming in the nighttime forest. Now we're not afraid of wolves, bears, or mountain lions because for we've shooed them out of our cities and towns. And for the most part we've put them on reservations—wildlife sanctuaries, preserves, national parks—where we can enjoy their wildness safely. We've made them afraid of us.

But we must miss them. We invite their tame relatives—dogs and cats, as well as birds, bunnies, ferrets, and fish—into our homes, to cuddle, to play with us, to eat our food, even to doze alongside of us when we sleep. We are comforted by their presence. We love them.

I know whereof I speak. Whenever I settle down to read or write or watch a movie, I am aware that Kaylee is somewhere nearby quietly watching over me. Cosmo is also nearby watching over me, though she's not quiet. They keep me happy. Mary, however, is not nearby. She is usually in the bedroom watching over her dog biscuits.

CHAPTER 61

Hormones

AFTER BREAKFAST TODAY Cosmo looked at me directly in the eye and bit my thumb.

"Ow!" I exclaimed.

"That's bad bird?" Cosmo asked casually in her usual soft, sweet voice.

"Yes, Cosmo! That's bad bird."

Cosmo bit me again, a little harder.

"Time to go back in cage," I said.

"Time to go back in cage," she repeated. I incarcerated her. She started whistling "Yankee Doodle." Cosmo never feels bad after being bad.

In no time she promised, "Cosmo wanna be a good bird. Cosmo don't bite. Okay? Cosmo wanna go up."

Sometimes when she's done something against house rules Cosmo chuckles as I put her "back in cage."

This morning Cosmo knew perfectly well she was being a bad bird. And she knew how I would react to her little bite. She bit to get a rise out of me, not to hurt me. She was not angry. She was not protecting her cage. She was having fun. She was challenging my authority.

At least that's what I think.

Experts knowledgeable about avian sexual behavior may think otherwise, however. They may attribute her anti-authoritarian behavior to hormonal changes.

Parrots, both male and female, have a reputation among us humans for moodiness, which experts explain as a normal response to their body's reproductive cycle.

Here's what I've learned about the reproductive cycle of female parrots. A female parrot is initially endowed with two ovaries, like mammals. But unlike mammals, the female parrot's right ovary shrinks after she hatches, and her left ovary, which contains all the eggs she will ever produce, enlarges. Her hormones stimulate her ovarian activity—her egg-laying—as well as her preparations ahead of time to be a good wife and a good mother.

In wild African grey parrots, hormonal changes are predictable because breeding is seasonal, and their reproductive urges are satisfied. In pet parrots like Cosmo, who is celibate, hormonal changes are unpredictable and their reproductive urges are not satisfied.

Cosmo could be exhibiting the behavior a female grey exhibits when she is ready to mate. That is, the search for dark places to make a nest, affectionate regurgitation of food, and aggressiveness. All this week Cosmo has disappeared into the towel cabinet every time I've left open the bathroom door. Yesterday Cosmo regurgitated a cashew for me. In the evening she cuddles one minute and nips me the next. But that's not unusual for her.

I wonder about this moodiness theory. I can't imagine a dove being irritable or a possum being grouchy at a particular time of the year. Or a wild African Grey being in a bad mood.

I suspect that many parrots are moody not because of hormones, or not solely because of hormones, but because of being confined in a cage under the power of humans instead of being free to fly through the rain forest with other birds of their own kind. They are experiencing natural reproductive urges in an environment that is not natural.

Parrots are highly sociable, smart animals who need flock mates, intellectual excitement, and some freedom to explore their world and follow their own impulses. Periodically Cosmo asserts her independence from me. She deliberately disobeys me, hides from me, or tells me "no!" when I've invited her to do something. Or she bites me. I consider her behavior to be normal, in view of her accommodation to the demands I make of her in the environment I've given her.

Now Cosmo's raising a ruckus, going "beep beep beep beep beep" like a truck backing up, and laughing loudly. She just called out to me "I'm here!" as if I were wondering, and asked "Here are you?" Then she called out to the crows alighting on the deck railing, "Caw caw caw."

Now she's telling me, "Cosmo wanna be a good bird" and "I love you!"

If we parrot-lovers want to keep parrots, whose natural behavior not even the parrots themselves can easily control, we need to accommodate their disposition. After all, they are birds. They fly, when they can, to the beat of a different drummer.

CHAPTER 62

Big Brain

HAVE YOU EVER TRIED TO GET DRESSED with a parrot clinging to your wrist? It's impossible! Or almost impossible.

First, if your parrot is on your left wrist, you have to hold your blouse with your left hand and put your right arm into the right sleeve. Then you have to switch the parrot from your left wrist to your right wrist and put your left arm into the left sleeve. Then you have to button your blouse with the parrot bobbing up and down as you use both hands to maneuver the buttons into the buttonholes. You try to keep your parrot from grabbing a button, or your necklace, with her beak.

Cosmo loves me so much she sometimes refuses to get off my wrist.

I do the laundry and the dishes with Cosmo hanging on, and I open jars and bottles. Occasionally Cosmo chuckles.

I wonder what is going on in her little brain.

Actually it's not so little for a bird. Parrots have big brains relative to the size of their body. In fact, parrots and crows have a brain-to-body size ratio comparable to that of chimpanzees and gorillas.

Neurobiologists have discovered that parrots, crows and other Corvids, and songbirds have a higher density of neurons in their forebrain than other birds and actually as many neurons as primates have.

Neurobiologist Pavel Nmec at Charles University in Prague said, "This pretty much answers the question we began with: How can these birds be so clever with such small brains? . . . . The answer is that there are so many neurons, their computing power is comparable to that of primates."

McGill University animal behaviorist Louis Lefebvre, who finds a correlation between brain size and intelligence, has developed an "innovativeness" index to measure a bird's IQ. He defines intelligence as the ability to adapt to different challenges, and he ranks crows the highest.

Before coming to that conclusion, Lefebvre collected bird stories from around the world. Among them is the account of the Japanese Carrion crows who place walnuts in front of tires when cars are stopped for a red light, and then they recover the crushed nuts after the cars roll over them.

I would give the African grey high marks for intelligence, but I'm happy to have the crow be valedictorian. I like crows and ravens as well as all species of parrots.

Cockatoos have acquired fame not only for unlocking their own cages but also for picking a series of locks with no prior training. Alex Kacelnik and colleagues at the University of Oxford challenged cockatoos to figure out how to open transparent doors locked with multiple locks. Pippin, the most skillful of the five birds, manipulated pins, bolts, screws, levers, latches, and wheels in the correct order to unlock the door. He could do this repeatedly, even when the locks were re-set in different positions.

Cosmo seeks new challenges to overcome and problems to solve. One challenge was to pick the latch of the closet in my bathroom. She took it completely apart, but she didn't actually break it. I couldn't put it back together, but my handyman could.

She has already solved the problem of taking apart pens without breaking them.

One day Cosmo hurried into my study from her room. I picked her up and then looked at her feet. Oh, no! Was she bleeding?

"Cosmo!" I exclaimed. "What did you do?"

"Hi," she said.

I carried her with me back into her room, not knowing what I'd find. But no glass, no blood. Thank goodness. Only a big, irregular stain of red ink seeping into the floor. Cosmo had dismantled the red pen that I kept at the back of the second shelf of my telephone stand.

CHAPTER 63

Natural and Unnatural

"I HAVE A LITTLE SHADOW that goes in and out with me."

That line from Robert Louis Stevenson's poem "My Shadow" entered my thoughts this morning as Cosmo followed me down the hall to the kitchen. I'd offered to give her a ride from the bedroom, but she'd refused.

Cosmo had asked me, "Betty Jean gonna go to kitch?" She abbreviates "kitchen."

"Yes, Cosmo," I replied. "I'm gonna go to kitchen. Do you wanna go to kitchen?"

"Noooo," she said. "Cosmo wanna stay here."

But Cosmo changed her mind. As I left the bedroom, I heard her clamber down the side of the cage and hurry down the hall behind me. Tic tac tic tac tic tac. I didn't turn around. When she caught up with me she said, "Hi!" She knew I'd be happy to see her. I was.

When Cosmo follows me—and that's often—she does it on foot. Tic tac tic tac. Don't worry. She can certainly keep up. She scurries faster than I walk.

I have Cosmo's flight feathers clipped for her own well-being. She could lose her life if she flew into a window or out the door, as she could easily do in my house. Since she is my precious housemate, I want to keep her safe.

However, the practice of clipping a parrot's flight feathers has critics as well as advocates. The issue is complex, for both critics and advocates make good arguments based on ethical considerations. Both want what's best for the parrot.

Critics of flight-feather clipping argue that we humans are unnecessarily depriving our feathered companions of one of their innate abilities, one of their innate pleasures: flying.

They say it's not natural for a parrot to have to walk everywhere. They have a point.

Advocates of the practice ask whether it's natural for a parrot to fly through a house rather than through a rain forest. Cosmo lives with a human and two dogs instead of parrots of her own kind, and she uses words to communicate instead of bird calls. Is that natural?

If we define a natural life for a parrot as a life without humans, very little about Cosmo's life is natural. But what's natural anyway?

What about a dog's life? How natural is it? More than ten thousand years ago we humans selectively bred wolves to create dogs to guard us, herd our sheep, pull our sleds, sit on our laps, and love us. Are dogs unnatural?

Frosty, a fifteen-pound bichon frisé who walks with my dogs Kaylee and Mary on Sundays, spends his evenings on the lap of his human Joan. Is Frosty less natural than his wolfish ancestors? By the way, Frosty has been neutered, and Mary and Kaylee have been spayed.

Are pigs natural? Farmers created them nine thousand years ago by artificial selection.

What about the beautiful voodoo hybrid tea rose?

Is birth control natural?

One spring Cosmo almost died from having an egg stuck in her reproductive tract. The condition of egg-binding could have caused infection had the egg broken inside her, or it could have caused nerve damage or death. Cosmo's life was saved by avian veterinarians at the University of Georgia College of Veterinary Medicine, who immediately put Cosmo on birdy birth control.

Humans have habitually categorized as "natural" everything on the planet that we are not intentionally manipulating, in contrast with what we are doing intentionally. Accordingly, we think of Antarctica as natural; New York City as not; the rain forest as natural; the greenhouse as not.

But, truth be told, we humans have manipulated both Antarctica and the rain forest whether intentionally or unintentionally, for our activities have affected all parts of the Earth's ecosystem.

Witness the jet trails in our skies.

And we have manipulated our bodies. We not only use birth control, but we also use pharmaceuticals to prolong our lives many years beyond what our ancestors enjoyed. And we have acquired the technical ability to modify our genomes.

Our age-old dualism of natural and unnatural is a cultural fiction. We're all part of nature. The concept "unnatural" is as antiquated today as the assumption that there is only one right way to be.

But even though unpolluted "nature" might be a fantasy, the concept can serve a valuable purpose. It reminds us of what we are destroying with our conversion of almost everything on Earth into commodities for ourselves.

I like thinking that we living organisms compose a grand family, all of us interrelated and interactive, nobody more natural or less natural than anybody else.

Back to parrots. Humans have lived with parrots for at least twenty-five hundred years. When we bring them into our homes, we and they become interrelated and interactive. We influence their lives, and they influence ours. Our pet birds develop their personalities as members of our families, and we develop ours as their companions and caregivers. We humans become kinder and wiser by our love for them, just as we do by our love for our dogs and our other pets.

Whenever my friends praise Cosmo by telling her, "Cosmo is a good bird, Cosmo is a pretty bird, Cosmo has beautiful feathers," Cosmo spreads her wings proudly. Cosmo does not know she's been physically modified to live in my house. She knows only that we think she's "a good bird." And that we love her.

CHAPTER 64

Many Worlds

"IT'S RAINING," SAID COSMO. She was right. The skies were dark, and rain was pounding the deck.

Cosmo keeps me abreast of what's happening around our house. She was perched atop her roost cage in our sunroom. I was reading.

Suddenly a tree limb hit the roof. Thud.

"What's that?" Cosmo asked.

"I don't know," I replied. How could I explain to her the effect of storm winds on tree limbs?

Mary and Kaylee started barking in the bedroom. Cosmo commented, "Doggies bark," descended from her perch, and hurried across the hall to see what was up.

"Hi," Cosmo said to the dogs.

So cute, I thought. Cosmo thinks she's important.

Then I realized how patronizing I was being. From Cosmo's perspective, the house is hers as much as mine. The dogs are her friends as much as mine. She speaks with me in English not to be cute but to communicate. From her perspective, I'm part of her life, but I'm not in charge of her life.

Cosmo doesn't know I'm supporting her. Or that I purchased her for my entertainment. Or that she, like other domestically-raised parrots, was bred to be a pet for people who like talking birds.

I'm reminded of a lesson I got from one of my favorite books: Ishmael, by Daniel Quinn. The novel is narrated by a philosophically–inclined student of a philosophically–inclined gorilla named Ishmael. In the course of their dialogue, the student figures out that civilized humans act as though the planet belongs to us. For more than two thousand years, we have viewed all of nature as ours to conquer, possess, exploit, use, and consume. We have viewed ourselves as Earth's only intelligent creatures.

We dominated Earth's other inhabitants because we considered that to be our right, our responsibility, and our destiny.

In the seventeenth century, under the assumption that only humans had consciousness and the ability to feel pain, French philosopher René Descartes dissected live dogs without administering painkiller. For Descartes, animals were like machines.

In the nineteenth century, Charles Darwin upended this assumption by showing us that humans and non-humans are related evolutionarily and that we consequently have much in common anatomically and behaviorally.

Enter YouTube in 2005. YouTube will forever change the public's ideas about nature, I'm convinced. Look at these videos of animals behaving like us or rather as I'd prefer to describe them, videos of humans and non-human all behaving like each other.

One video, titled "Amazing Squirrel Fights Off Crows," shows a very agitated squirrel trying to keep three crows from eating the remains of a fellow squirrel just killed by a car. Outnumbered by the hungry crows, the squirrel resorts to lying on top of her dead friend's body to protect it.

Incidentally, when Cosmo watched that video with me she focused on the crows. "That's birdie," she said. I had focused on the squirrels.

Another video, titled "Bird mourning over friend," shows a pigeon nervously staying right by the side of a dead pigeon lying in the street. The pigeon circles the body of his fallen friend again and again.

A third video, titled "60min clip4 elephant funeral," shows several elephants frantically attempting to revive a dead infant, poking the baby elephant with their trunks and trying to get him back up. Once they realize their baby is dead, they file solemnly past the body in an apparent funeral procession.

When we watch such videos we understand their behavior because of its similarity to ours. We hardly think about our differences.

Now that we know that mammals and birds mourn the death of their friends and family, develop emotional attachments to each other, and in ways we don't yet understand, communicate with each other, shouldn't we humans expand the community in which we do unto others as would have others do unto us?

Whose world is it, anyway? It's not just ours.

CHAPTER 65

Boundaries

ONE MORNING COSMO WAS PERCHED behind me in my study whistling joyfully when something raced across the roof, startling both of us.

"What's that?" Cosmo and I asked each other simultaneously. We think alike, I guess. At least we turn to each other for information about our environment. Cosmo and I both know what to expect in the way of sights and sounds around here.

"That's squirrel," I answered. It wasn't the season or time of day for reindeer.

Then Cosmo left my study, scurried down the hall, went into the sunroom, and stood by the glass door to observe the wildlife activity on the deck up close—though from six inches off the ground and from inside the house.

The doves, crows, and cardinals who live in the woods here year-round as well as the migrating hummingbirds, robins, and goldfinches who don't, enjoy a freedom that neither Cosmo nor I enjoy, the freedom to go where they wanna go, do what they wanna do.

Cosmo doesn't have such freedom because she is a pet. A pet, according to the *American Heritage Dictionary*, is "an animal kept for amusement or companionship." Cosmo has limitations on her travel. Her freedom to travel is constrained by the walls of our house.

I too have limitations on my travel. I am constrained by national borders, like all human residents of our subdivided Earth.

Wild birds don't know anything about national borders. They don't know when they're leaving Mexico and entering the United States. Nobody stops them. They are not citizens of any country or captives of any people. They can fly wherever they feel the need to go—to migrate, to search for food, to find a mate.

You'd expect that all wild animals would have the same freedom. But non-flying residents of Earth—deer, possums, armadillos, foxes, bear, turtles, etc.—don't. Their travel is limited by our Interstate Highway System. If in their search for food or a mate they don't stay within the regions bordered by our highways, we run over them with our cars.

Think about the pronghorns. Pronghorns are hoofed mammals, among the world's fastest, who stand about three feet tall at the shoulder. For six thousand years pronghorns have migrated back and forth from the Grand Tetons in Wyoming, where they spend the summer, to the Upper Green River Valley, some hundred fifty miles south, where they spend the winter. Over the past one hundred years, humans have crisscrossed their pathway with highways and fences, threatening their survival by impeding their migration. Now some conservation groups, alarmed by the depletion of their population, are trying to protect them.

When we construct boundaries such as highways and fences that enclose wild animals in smaller and smaller spaces, shrinking their gene pool, depriving them of the freedom their ancestors enjoyed, and then, belatedly, taking them into our care, are we unintentionally turning them into our outdoor pets?

Over time I suspect the possums north of I-20 will look a little different from the possums south of I-20. We won't detect the differences, but the possums will if the I-20 barrier ever comes down and the southern possums and their long-forgotten northern relatives reunite.

Cosmo doesn't worry about events beyond her life span. She notices only departures from routine. All animals, human and non-human alike, notice just the unusual, immediately discernible changes in our environment, as we work and play

211

Hide and seek.

through the days of our lives. Only by gathering knowledge about the long-term changes underway in our planetary ecosystem can we learn the consequences of our activity on Earth's other residents.

While writing this column, I pulled up the Mamas and the

Papas song "Go Where You Wanna Go." The music erupted from my computer because the volume was up.

Cosmo cried out from her room, "What's that?" The blast of sound was certainly a departure from our household routine.

I replied, "That's music."

CHAPTER 66

Ranking

THIS MORNING COSMO AND I played hide-and-seek.

"Cosmoooo! Where are you?" I called out.

Cosmo was hiding in the cabinet under the sink. When I entered the bathroom, she poked her head out, exclaimed, "There you are!" and scurried into the bedroom and under the bed. I chased her unsuccessfully. She scurries faster than I walk.

I begged her, "Cosmo, come here! Please!"

Cosmo stayed out of sight. She chuckled.

Finally, I went into the hall where I couldn't be seen. I heard her tic tac tic tac across the hardwood floor. I returned to the bedroom.

Now Cosmo was hiding behind the toilet peering through a hole in its base.

"Wanna come here?" she asked. Then she pulled away out of sight, and chuckled.

I tell stories like this one to audiences interested in animal intelligence. Often people ask: "Is the African grey the smartest bird in the world?" and "Is the African grey the smartest animal in the world?" Once, "Is the African grey smarter than a German Shepherd?"

Cosmo is unlike a German Shepherd in that she can use human speech to make her wishes known. Dogs can't. But that doesn't mean that Cosmo is smarter than a German Shepherd. She's simply different.

In Western civilization we've inherited a habit of ranking that we can trace back to Aristotle in Greek Antiquity. Twenty-five hundred years ago Aristotle described nature in terms of a "scale of ascent" and inclined us thereafter to rank what we saw.

We ranked the races and the sexes: whites higher than yellows, reds, and blacks; males higher than females.

We ranked the animals on the basis of their resemblance to us. We ranked humans higher than chimps and gorillas, whom we ranked higher than cows and pigs, whom we ranked higher than woodrats and gophers, whom we ranked higher than bees and plankton.

The lower the animal's rank the better we felt about eating him, experimenting on him, or polluting his habitat.

In 1734 poet Alexander Pope described the hierarchy as a "Great Chain of Being," an unchanging natural order that he said humans shouldn't question.

But in 1859 Charles Darwin questioned it in *On the Origin of Species*, where he showed that nature changed continuously and that species evolved. Since then biologists have taught us that there's no fixed order in nature, that difference among Earth's creatures does not mean difference in value, and that nature is more like a web than a ladder.

In 1953, in his textbook *Fundamentals of Ecology*, University of Georgia ecologist Eugene Odum developed the concept of the ecosystem. Succeeding generations of ecology students in many countries learned that the components of an ecosystem are all interactive and are all important to its stability.

We now think of Earth as a planetary ecosystem, in which everybody, including woodrats, has a valuable job to do. We now consider bees and plankton as essential to the biosphere as cuddly animals with cute faces. We now see the value of all the parts of a whole—whether it's a nation, an ecosystem, or our global society—because all parts interact with each other to keep the system healthy.

We advocate universal human rights, and we appreciate diversity in culture and nature. Everybody matters.

I hope that one day we will shed this habit of ranking folks according to our human kind of intelligence, which we think we can measure by tests.

There are all kinds of intelligence. Within humankind,

there's the mathematician kind, the musician kind, the writer kind, the athlete kind, the fireman kind, the mother kind, the loving, charming, generous, thoughtful friend kind.

And then there's the African Grey kind of intelligence, the German Shepherd kind, the woodrat kind, the hummingbird kind.

Don't forget the starling kind. On a YouTube video there is a glorious murmuration of starlings swooping and swirling across the twilight sky over the River Shannon. The thousands of birds, maybe hundreds of thousands, have migrated to the United Kingdom to escape the frigid winters of Russia and Scandinavia. They know their way. And they know how to fly together, very closely together.

The starlings appear to be flying in unison, but actually they are not. Nor are they following a leader. Each bird monitors the movements of the seven birds flying nearest him and responds in a millisecond to any bird's change of direction. That's how the starlings escape their predators. To the human eye, the flock changes direction instantaneously.

These starlings have mental abilities that humans don't have and can't imagine.

I think of William Butler Yeats's line "How can we know the dancer from the dance?" The single starling perched on a branch gives us no inkling of what she does in murmuration.

In my view, intelligence is not a thing to have or not to have. Intelligence cannot be measured. Intelligence makes itself known through behavior. It is nothing if not employed. A dancer is a dancer when dancing.

Is an African grey smarter than a German Shepherd? Smarter than a starling? I say there's no answer to that question because the question's not right. Let's ask instead what different animals and different individuals can do with the minds they have.

Cosmo has made me realize we have underestimated the

mental abilities of birds and probably everybody else with whom we share Earth's bounty. As we change our views of other beings, we will change our behavior toward them, and maybe toward each other.

It is seven o'clock and dark. Cosmo just asked me. "Time to go to kitchen?"

"Yes, Cosmo," I told her. "It's time to go to kitchen." Cosmo has adapted to my schedule in my home. That shows mental flexibility. Could I adapt to hers if we lived together in the rain forest?

Chapter 67

Cages

YESTERDAY AFTERNOON WHILE PREPARING DINNER I dropped a heavy glass lid on my ankle.

"*¡Ay, caramba!*" I exclaimed in pain.

Cosmo, watching me from her perch atop her dining room cage, immediately asked, "Cosmo bad bird?" Then she said "Cosmo go back in cage," descended from her perch, and entered her cage.

Poor Cosmo! She is so often in trouble, so often the cause of my exclamations of distress, that she figured she'd done something wrong again. She took the blame for the accident.

Cosmo usually wants free range of my house. But she does not consider her cage a jail cell. In fact, she loves to play cage games with me. While perched atop the cage in my bedroom she'll announce "Cosmo wanna kiss-feathers," and then, laughing loudly, retreat into the cage when I move toward her. The cage is her private space, and I'm supposed to keep out.

Once she pulled the cage door shut to keep me out.

Cosmo's cages are large. The interior measures twenty-nine inches high, twenty-four inches wide, and twenty-two inches deep. When Cosmo perches on top she's almost six feet off the floor. But parrot cages have not always been this spacious.

I googled "antique bird cages" and found cages shockingly small even for a canary. Many nineteenth-century cages were only fifteen inches high, and not as wide. They were objects of beauty to adorn elegant homes, as were the birds they housed.

Next, I googled "bird cage history" and discovered a book published in London in 1871 called *A Natural History of Cage*

Birds, by John Gerrard Keulemans. It began: "Of all the foreign cage-birds that decorate and enliven our dwellings, few are more common or better known than the Grey Parrot."

Oh, no! Cosmo's relatives lived in those tiny cages.

Then Keulemans told with great excitement how in 1865 he had killed and captured grey parrots. In western Africa where he owned a plantation, Mr. Keulemans and a "native" had cut their way through a jungle to reach the greys' roosting place. He wrote:

"My gratification at this moment was extreme. What should be done? Shoot as many of the old birds as presented themselves, or seek out their nests and take the young ones home?"

In the end he took home six living parrots, three dead ones, and one egg.

Then Keulemans gave advice to owners of grey parrots: "If, while being taught to imitate words or sounds, the bird exhibits an indifference or unwillingness to learn its lesson, it will be found of service to cover the cage with a dark-coloured cloth."

Yikes! Darkness awaited the poor captive grey who didn't perform for his human master.

But Keulemans's attitude toward birds and other animals was not unusual for his time.

Nineteenth-century Europeans and Americans tended to think of humans as special creations, absolutely distinct from the rest of nature. They generally considered "nature" as something external to themselves to be dominated, controlled, owned, or used for their benefit. In their view, nature belonged to humans. They put fancy birds into fancy cages to make fancy living rooms. And when they encountered attractive animals in the wild, they felt little guilt over capturing or shooting them.

There were outstanding exceptions, among them John Jay Audubon and Ernst Haeckel, who drew the plants, birds, and other animals they loved, and Charles Darwin, who figured out how the plants, birds, and other animals evolved. Haeckel gave the name of "ecology" to the discipline that emerged after Darwin focused our attention on the interconnectedness of nature's organisms.

Audubon, Haeckel, and Darwin influenced our present-day appreciation of nature. Now environmentalists are showing us that nature does not belong to humans. Rather, humans belong to nature. We humans, the birds and bees, flowers and trees, bears and whales, algae and plankton, soil, water, and air are all essential components of Earth, inter-related, interactive, and interdependent.

We have the same molecules, differently arranged. Humans and the other animals with whom we live in our planetary ecosystem are not altogether different from each other.

That's what I think of when I listen to Peter, Paul, and Mary sing "There is only one river, there is only one sea, and it flows through you, and it flows through me." Peter Yarrow wrote that lovely song, "River of Jordan," in 1972.

CHAPTER 68

Fluorescence

THIS MORNING I ACCIDENTALLY BUMPED Cosmo's T-stand and startled her off her perch. She flew to the ground ten feet away and said, "Ooooh," as I would have under similar circumstances.

Cosmo looked up at me. Following my natural instincts, I lifted her from the floor and brought her to my chest. There, with her tiny heart pounding, Cosmo lay quietly against me and closed her eyes in anticipation of my caresses.

After a couple of minutes of blissful cuddling, Cosmo yanked my necklace and broke the spell.

"Wanna talk?" she asked.

Was Cosmo following her natural instincts when she relaxed under my gentle hand? I doubt it. The desire to cuddle would hardly be advantageous to an African Grey in the rainforests of the Congo. Cosmo's cuddliness seems to be my creation. Like her speech.

I'm typing with my right hand now because Cosmo won't let go of my left. Is this natural?

The question of what's natural and what's not has become obviously inappropriate in the twenty-first century. I have no idea how to classify talking parrots, and chickens, pigs, milk cows, two-headed turtles, five-legged frogs, fish high on antidepressants that have leached into their stream, and fluorescent animals. They all show human handiwork.

Genetic engineers can create florescent animals. They simply inject somebody with fluorescent genes, which they get from ocean critters such as jellyfish and sea anemone. And voilà, they get sheep, rabbits, pigs, cats, marmosets, dogs, chickens, whatever, who glow under a black light.

By the way, transgenic marmosets have passed on their fluorescence to their offspring. So have transgenic dogs.

Many species of parrots fluoresce without any genetic help from us humans because their feathers have florescent pigment. But until scientists put parrot feathers under a black light we didn't know it because we don't see ultraviolet colors. Parrots see ultraviolet colors and therefore notice each other's fluorescence. Zoologist Kathryn Arnold of the University of Glasgow reports that the budgies who fluoresce most brightly attract the most potential mates. Fluorescence makes parrots sexy.

I can imagine that humans will want the same courtship advantages that the sexy, fluorescent parrots have. Before long television ads for Viagra and Botox will be accompanied by ads for injections of fluorescent genes. "Ask your doctor whether this is right for you," a seductive male voice will intone as glowing young men and women share a romantic dinner over a black light. Love is available with just one shot.

"Glo-with-the-Fluo" injections, expensive at $999, will become a must-have for everybody seeking courtship success. Soon fluorescent folks will marry other fluorescent folks and have fluorescent children who will have fluorescent parrots, pups, and pigs for pets. They'll live in black-lighted neighborhoods and will grill fluorescent chicken in the dark on their fluorescent lawns. They'll have bright teeth.

That doesn't seem natural. Some non-transgenic folks will disapprove.

Yet the fluorescent genes in the transgenic humans came out of fluorescent jellyfish and sea anemone, who were certainly natural.

Maybe we should forget about judging what's natural and what's not.

Maybe we should just distinguish between organic and non-organic when the difference matters, as when we're shopping for food to put into our bodies.

After much thought about the subject, I conclude that all

Earth's organisms are natural. Even two-headed turtles and five-legged frogs. Even medicated fish and medicated humans and humans with faux teeth and knees. Even transgenic humans and transgenic pigs.

After all, we wouldn't want to treat a transgenic pig as if he were not as worthy of respect as any other pig. He didn't ask to be made that way.

If we don't inspect everybody with a black light, we won't even know who's transgenic.

Now I look at Cosmo in a new way. Her body feathers are many shades of gray, and her tail feathers are scarlet—at least as I perceive them. I don't know whether she glows. I consider her beautiful because I see her beautiful soul. I know her up close and personal, and I love her. I wonder whether other parrots would consider her just sexy.

CHAPTER 69

Animals on Television

THIS MORNING WHEN I WAS GETTING READY to leave the house I called out "Cosmo, where are you?"

I looked under the bed, where she likes to hide with Mary and Kaylee. I looked in my closet where she likes to perch on the clothes hamper. I looked in the bathroom on the counter, under the sink, in the towel closet, and in my cosmetic drawers, which were ajar.

"Cosmo, where are you?" I asked again.

"Hi!" Cosmo piped up from behind me.

There she was, standing proudly on the rim of the bathtub. She'd ascended via the drawers she'd pulled open.

Cosmo scrambled around to the other side of the tub where I couldn't reach her. She chuckled. I let her stay there to explore her new territory, for she was obviously having fun. A minute later I heard a flutter of wings and then a plaintive plea.

"Come here! Cosmo wanna go up!" She'd slid into the bathtub, and she couldn't get out. She needed my help.

This time Cosmo stepped submissively onto my hand.

Cosmo trusts that I will care for her whether she's being good or bad, and rescue her when she's in trouble. She needs me, and she knows it. And I know it. I want her to be happy, as well as healthy.

I want all the animals over whom humans have power to have a lifetime of health and happiness. Even the chickens and cows we plan to eat. Now that we've been told by neuroscientists that birds and mammals have consciousness, we have a moral obligation, I believe, to include them in our ethical community.

I've been asking myself why animal protection has recently become such a hot topic for ethicists, and animal cognition such a hot field for researchers. I've concluded that Hollywood deserves some credit for awakening us to our unintentional neglect and abuse of the animals who share our space on Earth. Since Walt Disney's *Steamboat Willie* in 1928, cartoons, movies, and television programs have influenced us to empathize with animals we may have never observed.

Think about Disney cartoons. My friend Richard Neupert, a University of Georgia film scholar, has pointed out that Walt Disney got children to identify with his extraordinarily cute animals in extraordinarily interesting predicaments by making his cartoons realistic, well, at least more realistic than those of his competitors in the 1930s.

Disney made Mickey Mouse, who wore white gloves, big yellow shoes, and red shorts, and Donald Duck, who wore a sailor suit, the protagonists of realistic stories. Disney placed them in realistic landscapes, where ponds had ripples and trees cast shadows. Disney gave them human-like personalities, with emotions and ideas children understood. He gave them expressive faces and natural, though exaggerated, body movements. He made his characters part of a society.

Children loved Mickey, Donald, Henny Penny, Chicken Little, Foxy Loxy, Bambi, Thumper, Flower, Dumbo, and Br'er Bear.

Now think about all the non-animated films that have shaped our understanding of particular animals: *Jungle Book, Flipper, Born Free, Never Cry Wolf, Gorillas in the Mist, Paulie, March of the Penguins,* and *The Wild Parrots of Telegraph Hill.* And *Jaws.*

Think of all the educational programs that have appeared on Nature Channel, Discovery, National Geographic, and of course PBS. Sesame Street regularly shows short clips of animals in the wild. Thus very young Sesame Street fans are acquainted with warthogs, wombats, orangutans, hippopotamuses, aardvarks, and flamingos.

For close to a century we've seen on the screen animals we've not seen in the flesh, and we think we know those animals. We like them, we talk about them, we want to preserve their habitats, and we want to treat them kindly, even those we ultimately turn into dinner. I hope that before another century passes, we humans will extend human kindness to everybody.

CHAPTER 70

Animal Experimentation

A FRIEND ALERTED ME to a YouTube video of a Beluga whale imitating the human voice. When I played it Cosmo asked, "What's that?"

The whale sounded human. I replied, "That's a whale wanna talk."

Cosmo was monitoring my activity on my computer from her perch behind me. She prefers YouTubes of birds but she watches dogs, cats, and elephants and whatever else I pull up in the way of animals.

She especially likes the YouTube of herself taking a dip in the doggies' water bowl. See her channel: http://www.YouTube.com/user/cosmotalks.

The young whale, named NOC, was mimicking the human conversations he had overheard among the divers in his tank at the National Marine Mammal Foundation in San Diego. Scientists attribute NOC's behavior to whales' long vocal-learning period. NOC learned his calls from the humans in his tank, not from his biological mother, not from a pod of whale pals.

Four years later, upon reaching maturity, NOC abandoned his human-ish speech and thereafter emitted only normal whale sounds.

When I think of humans keeping whales in tanks, chimps in research institutes, mice in laboratories, and other animals in zoos, all to satisfy our curiosity, I feel bad. We are sentencing sensitive individuals to lifetimes of unhappiness in order to acquire knowledge about their species.

I also admit I'm keeping Cosmo in my home to satisfy my curiosity about her species, as well as to have a feathery little friend.

How can we justify incarceration of individuals of any species? For more than ten thousand years humans have exploited other animals, not just for food but for transportation, protection, work, entertainment, and companionship. For more than twenty-five hundred years, at least since Aristotle, we have used animals for scientific experimentation.

Of course, we weren't seeing the world from the animals' viewpoint. Our ability to dominate other species reinforced our conviction that the human species was superior, specially created, absolutely different from every other species, and unique in having consciousness. And conversely, our belief in our human superiority justified our domination of the less powerful.

Question: Why should we twenty-first-century humans behave differently from our predecessors?

Answer: Because we understand animals in ways our predecessors did not.

We've started seeing the world from the animals' perspective. And how did we acquire this new understanding? Paradoxically, our very experimentation on animals has shown us their sensitivity to pain, their capacity for emotional suffering, and their intelligence. It has prompted our obligation to treat them with respect and kindness, prevent their suffering, and preserve their habitat.

I still feel bad for NOC, who had the misfortune to be captured. Yet by isolating NOC from other Belugas, scientists learned enough about the whale's mental agility to prick our consciences and make us question our treatment of animals in captivity. The scientists' research on NOC may influence us to save the whales. That is, save them in "the wild." That is, if there is any wild anymore.

I am heartened by all the legislation passed recently to protect the animals with whom we share our planet, even the animals we eat, even the animals we put in zoos, even the animals we subject to experimentation, even the animals we cast in movies. I am particularly glad that the Animal Care and Use

Office of the University of Georgia enforces not only the federal Animal Welfare Act Regulations but also the Public Health Service Policy on Humane Care and Use of Laboratory Animals, which protects all vertebrate animals.

The Animal Welfare Act excludes mice, agricultural animals, and most unfortunately, birds.

The purpose of animal use in research is to benefit not just the human species but other species too. The theory is that our incarceration of individual animals serves the well-being of their kin as well as humans.

Well, all I can say is that this ethical issue is certainly complicated.

While I write, Cosmo is trying to divert my attention by talking, barking, telling telephone jokes, and laughing. Now she is whistling a medley of tunes, tunes she learned from me, not from her mother, and not from other African Greys because she is not acquainted with any.

Cosmo pauses periodically to congratulate herself. "Wow, whatta bird!" She sends me kisses and says, "I love you!" I think she's happy. But I doubt that I could be as high spirited and affectionate as Cosmo if I were kept by a flock of parrots, even parrots who loved me and treated me royally as if I were one of them.

CHAPTER 71

Astrocytes

YESTERDAY AS I TOOK A SWEATER out of a drawer, Cosmo asked me, "That's clothes?"

Cosmo had generalized from my telling her over the years that "Cosmo has feathers. Cosmo is a birdie. Mary has fur. Mary is a doggie. Betty Jean has clothes."

So Cosmo really knew what "clothes" meant, whether they were on me or in a drawer.

Cosmo is a smart bird.

My friend Mark Farmer, a biologist at the University of Georgia, sent me an NPR report about some non-human animals being made less non-human. The report was titled "To Make Mice Smarter, Add a Few Human Brain Cells." I'll try to summarize it.

All brains have two kinds of cells: neurons, which emit electrical impulses, and glia, which surround and support the neurons. For more than a century, scientists have focused primarily on neurons, to the neglect of the abundant glia. However, neuroscientists have recently discovered that certain glial cells called astrocytes coordinate groups of neurons by chemical signals.

Astrocytes regulate the flow of information through the brain. The neurons of humans and non-animals look alike, but our astrocytes don't. Humans' astrocytes are bigger—that is, they have more extensions than all other creatures.

Steve Goldman of the University of Rochester wondered whether it's our astrocytes that make humans smarter than non-human animals. He and Maiken Medergaard injected some human astrocytes into the brains of newborn mice. The modified mice, who still looked and acted mousy, turned out to be smarter than the unmodified mice with only mouse astrocytes. The mice with human astrocytes learned faster on maze tests and made fewer mistakes.

Wow. Should we still classify the human-astrocyte mice as "non-human"?

What if the really smart mice decide they don't much like their caregivers, escape their lab, fall in love, and have sexual relations without protection? Let's imagine that they pass on their acquired intellectual prowess to their offspring and populate the world with intellectual human-astrocyte mice. Uh oh.

What if animal-friendly neuro-terrorists sneak into our barns and inject human astrocytes into the brains of newborn calves? When those calves grow up, will they decide they don't much like their caregivers, escape their farm, and populate the world with really smart, discontented, leftist cattle who will overthrow our factory farm industry? Under the leadership of Cow Marx and Ferdinand Engels they will moo "Cattle of the world, unite!"

What if neuro-terrorists sneak into our hospital nurseries and inject bovine astrocytes into human babies?

Humans have been tinkering with species since the agricultural revolution, which started some twelve thousand years ago. We've made dogs out of wolves. We've made pigs out of wild boar. We've made fancy pigeons. Google "Fancy Pigeon Gallery" to see a lot of very fancy pigeons locked up in tiny cages. If newly hatched fancy pigeons got human astrocytes they'd be outta there.

We have done all this by artificial selection—by deciding who mates with whom according to the traits we desire in the offspring. Darwin got his explanation for the origin of species from the principles of artificial selection. He was a pigeon fancier.

Only recently have scientists modified species by means other than selection. Genetic engineers have created hybrids we call GMOs, genetically modified organisms. In the future will astrocyte engineers make AMAs, astrocytically modified animals?

Cosmo is not a hybrid. African grey parrots evolved naturally, over millennia. I don't want curious researchers to inject human astrocytes into African greys to see what they'd do if they were smarter. The pet greys would probably be even more rebellious than they are now.

Last night Cosmo was quite rebellious.

I was getting dressed to go out when I noticed Cosmo enter the cabinet under my bathroom sink. "That's okay," I thought to myself. Cosmo can't damage anything there, and she can't get hurt.

A little later I opened the little drawer attached to the counter where I'd hidden my lipsticks from her. Oh my God! Iced Amethyst, Blue Rose, Iceblue Pink, Sea Fleur, and Gumdrop had all disappeared! The drawer was empty. Cosmo had accessed it from beneath the sink. I found the lipsticks in the waste basket where she'd dropped them, each lipstick open, each with deep beak marks.

"Cosmo!" I exclaimed.

"Cosmooooooo!" She mocked me. I parked her on the towel rack while I struggled to repair Iced Amethyst. She immediately tossed the towel onto the floor.

"Cosmo!" I exclaimed again.

"Cosmoooooo!" She mocked me again.

What would she do or say if she had human astrocytes in her brain?

Chapter 72

Connections

OCCASIONALLY I PUT COSMO ON HER T-STAND to keep her out of trouble.

The T-stand has food and water dishes on top, where she perches, but no ladder down to the floor. In other words, once Cosmo is on the stand, she has no access to books, telephone cords, baseboards, cosmetic drawers, or painted toenails. But she can be with me while I write, and she can watch YouTube.

What would I do without YouTube for my daily peek into the life of animals outside my home? Lately I've seen a parrot and a cat napping together, a monkey grooming a longhorn sheep, a dolphin kissing a dog, another dolphin flirting with a cat, a wolf touching the nose of an antelope, a dog communicating with a koi, a giraffe licking a squirrel, a chimp hugging a young puma, and a mouse climbing onto the back of a kitten. The web has made these inter-species affairs known to the world.

Images of animals making love, not war, appeal to us because they reinforce whatever dreams we have for peace and harmony and love all around. At least that's what they do for me. I look at those animals and think: They are like us. We're all like each other. We can get along.

We used to think of nature as "red in tooth and claw" characterized by "survival of the fittest." The poet Alfred Lord Tennyson and the philosopher Herbert Spencer gave us these aphorisms in the 19th century when our economic system inclined us to understand everything in terms of competition. We saw the world then as us–versus–them, and them–versu-them–others." Man–versus–nature. Every man for himself.

Win, or lose—in nature and in society.

But for some Americans who came of age in the 1960s, there's no longer any "them," either in nature or in society. Just "us." We're all "us."

This intellectual revolution came about in part because we learned in biology classes that humans, other animals, plants, soil, water, and air all interact with each other in ecosystems. The lesson, shocking to some, that we depend for our survival on earthworms, bees, bacteria, and plankton undermined our us–versus–them attitude toward nature.

Also folks of my generation were influenced by events. Remember these?

> Demonstrations for equal rights under the law for people of all races, religions, and ethnicities, for women, for the disabled;
> The Vietnam War;
> The anti-war music: "Come on people now, smile on your brother, everybody get together, and try to love one another right now" by The Youngbloods;
> The discovery that the DDT we sprayed to kill insects here on our farms brought harm to birds across the oceans, notably expressed by Rachel Carson in *Silent Spring* (1962);
> The lesson that our treatment of some of Earth's inhabitants affects others:
> The moon landing and the pictures from space of a beautiful planet with no visible fences, no national boundaries dividing Earth's people.

These events put the sense of connectivity into our heads. We now see ourselves as interconnected members of a global society and components of a planetary ecosystem. We're all hooked together. We may be different from each other, but in the bigger picture we are together, part of a whole. We are "us," ultimately inseparable.

When we see non-human animals, either in our homes or in the wild or on the web, we are more apt than previous generations to view them as part of our world, and we are more apt to view ourselves as part of theirs. In the twenty-first century, we are predisposed to find connections.

We like to encounter evidence of animal friendships, as in the photo of the parrot and the cat napping together, because we see that those animals are like us connecting with each other in close personal relationships. We identify with them.

I love to take my pets to the vet and hear the receptionist call out "Cosmo Craige," and "Mary Joy Craige," and "Kaylee Craige." A while back I'd hear "Sugar Bear Craige." Wow, I think, we belong together.

CHAPTER 73

Collaboration

I JUST DID MY LAUNDRY with Cosmo clinging to my left hand. Every time I leaned into the washer to pull out a garment Cosmo leaned over to peer in. Then she'd look at the garment and ask, "What's that?"

Cosmo loves to do household chores with me. And since she's figured out how to stay on my hand, we do more and more together. Like cleaning out the refrigerator and brushing my teeth, which we do together. I'm almost at the point of calling them "our" teeth.

By hanging out with me in this fashion, Cosmo has discovered what's in the refrigerator, the washer, the dryer, the linen closet, the clothes closet. She's discovered what's in every drawer and behind every door in the house, "our" house.

"I" don't do housework any more. "We," meaning "I" plus Cosmo, do housework. We entertain company together. We talk with each other, amuse each other, and make each other happy.

My Tanzanian friend Lioba Moshi, a linguist at the University of Georgia, told me over lunch about another interspecies relationship that benefits both parties.

On the savannas of East Africa, wildebeests and zebras form integrated herds. The wildebeests have poor eyesight and appreciate the company of the sharp-eyed zebras in daytime. And in nighttime the zebras, who have poor hearing, appreciate the company of the sharp-eared wildebeests, who also have a superior sense of smell. The wildebeests alert the herd to predators during the night, and the zebras alert the herd to predators during the day. The wildebeests and the zebras need each other. I'll bet they form interspecies friendships.

Many Tanzanians would liken the symbiosis of wildebeests and zebras to the way human society works.

Lioba told me that in local villages everybody helps each other. Nobody lives in isolation. If someone departs, he or she leaves behind an empty place. If someone dies, the whole village takes responsibility for the funeral and the care of the bereaved. If two get married, the whole village participates in the wedding, bringing food, drink, music, gifts.

Perhaps because those villages consider their members to be parts of the whole, the villagers view happiness not as an individual state of mind but as the result of a fortunate sequence of events in which others have participated. Villagers can't imagine being happy alone, for everybody is connected with others. "I" can't be happy all by myself, but "we" can be happy together.

Accordingly, individual self-sufficiency is not an ideal for African villagers. It's not an individual goal. It's not even an imaginable possibility. In the Tanzanians' symbiotic vision of the world, it takes a village, not just individual prowess, for anybody to thrive.

After lunch I thought about how very much our planet's cultures can learn from each other.

Musicians already know this. Paul Simon, whose concert collaborations with Hugh Masekela in apartheid South Africa, brought together blacks and whites in song and launched "world music."

Since I spend a lot of my waking hours contemplating furry and feathery animals, I liken the symbiosis of wildebeests and zebras to the way nature works.

Zebras and wildebeests can't talk, but if they could they'd probably refer to themselves as "we."

Cosmo can talk, but she says "I" and "Cosmo" a lot more often than "we." That's because she learned to speak from me. And though I try hard to think of all human and non-human animals as a great big "we," I belong to a culture where "I" have to take care of myself.

For the last ten minutes, Cosmo has been perched on my lap chomping on an emery board she found on my desk. I suddenly spotted a huge, ugly, scary inch-long centipede approaching my chair. I squealed. Cosmo leaned over to look as I stepped on it. When I lifted my foot I saw that I'd detached a leg from the centipede's body, and the leg was still moving!

I must have groaned because Cosmo groaned. Then Cosmo asked, "What's that?"

"That's a bug, Cosmo," I replied. "A bad, bad bug!"

And then I thought: That centipede and I are not "we"!

There goes my idealism.

CHAPTER 74

Emotional Life

"COSMO WANNA CUDDLE," Cosmo kept telling me last night, in her softest, sleepiest voice.

Cosmo was snuggling against my chest. I was caressing her head, neck, and back, and gently pulling her tail feathers. We were watching the movie My Cousin Vinnie, and we had already been cuddling for fifteen minutes. Her eyes were closed, but the instant I removed my hand from her little body to adjust the volume on the remote, she reminded me, "Cosmo wanna cuddle."

Cosmo was feeling affection for me. I am convinced.

I'll bet that anybody who has ever lived with a dog or a cat would be convinced.

Primatologist Frans de Waal of the Yerkes National Primate Research Center at Emory University, who worked for years with chimpanzees, would be likewise convinced. He wrote in Discover Magazine in 1997, "To endow animals with human emotions has long been a scientific taboo. But if we do not, we risk missing something fundamental, about both animals and us."

I agree with the distinguished professor.

Yet our language can lead us astray. If we say, "we have emotions," or "they don't have emotions," we have turned emotions into a thing to have or not have. Like feet.

Emotions are not a thing. They are no more a thing than alertness or hunger or fear. So instead of saying that we all have emotions, let's say that we all have an emotional life, which is a mental life. All of us, not just us humans.

And if we all have a mental life, we are all thinking and feeling all the time. We are thinking about one another. That's what humans and members of other species do.

Picture a family.

In a family, we're not all alike. Some of us are female, some male. Some big, some little. Some jolly, some solemn. Some Democrat, some Republican. Some of us have clothes, some have fur, some have feathers, some have scales.

If the family gets a new baby, a puppy, a parrot, or a boa constrictor, everybody's life is suddenly different from what it was before. The system has changed, but everybody is still hooked together.

In a family we're hooked together by blood, by love, by obligation, by the house we share, by our common history. When one of us budges, the others adjust. When one misbehaves, the others suffer. When one gets in trouble, the others help out. We need each other. Everybody matters.

And everybody is thinking about something.

Now picture a mixed-species family in Athens, Georgia. In my woods, as I write in late March, squirrels are figuring out how to steal seed from birdfeeders; finches are trying to claim the seed for themselves; owls are mating; foxes and possums are giving birth; turkey vultures are flying through the trees; deer are eating the corn put out for them by my neighbors; a mouse is trying to escape the talons of a hawk; the hawk is trying to catch the mouse to satisfy her hunger.

These animals are all individuals, interrelated individuals. And they are all thinking about something.

What if the process of thinking emitted a very, very, very, very faint hum that we could hear if we closed our eyes tight and listened with our imagination?

I can hear the humming. It's all around me. In the sky, in the trees, in the bushes, on the ground.

Now stop and listen to the humming of Earth's trillion interrelated individuals, each thinking about something. It's the sweet sound of the world a-turnin.

CHAPTER 75

Conclusion

I'M WATCHING TWO CROWS and a squirrel share the safflower seeds, sunflower seeds, thistle, corn, and peanuts I've put out on my deck railing. The squirrel had to move to the end when the crows alighted, but he didn't leave. The crows didn't try to scare him away either.

Spotting the crows, Cosmo has just scurried up to the sliding glass door, pecked at the glass, and called out, "That's birdie!"

I'm thinking, we are fam-i-ly!

We—not just humans but all of us residents of Earth, including birds—are family. We are interconnected, dependent upon each other, evolving in relation to each other. We share space on Earth, and we deserve to share Earth's bounty. That is one theme of *Ruminations on a Parrot Named Cosmo*.

The other theme of *Ruminations* is my discovery of a mind in a bird I love. I've told many anecdotes in this book about my dear Cosmo to show her mental life, her wit, her creativity, her cleverness, her affection for me, her resemblance to me. Cosmo is a smart, funny, loving individual to all who know her personally. I want my readers to know her too.

Cosmo is now eighteen years old. I've lived with her for almost a quarter of my life. She has enabled me to get a glimpse of the world from her viewpoint, to realize that the world does not belong to humans alone but also to a trillion other individuals with a lively mental life, individuals who don't feel subordinate to humans, individuals whose world is very different from ours.

Cosmo is also my friend.

When I was a little girl, I read a set of books by Thornton

Burgess that had belonged to my mother when she was a child. Thornton Burgess was a naturalist and conservationist who spent his life in Massachusetts from his birth in 1874 until his death in 1965. He told stories about woodland animals named Reddy Fox, Johnny Chuck, Jimmy Skunk, Little Joe Otter, Billy Mink, Jerry Muskrat, Bobby Coon, Chatterer the Squirrel, Uncle Billy Possum, Mr. Mocker, and Sammy Jay. I remember them all—not the stories, but the characters.

I lived in El Paso, Texas, where I could only fantasize about these animals I'd never seen who inhabited a forest far away. I wanted to grow up and live in the woods. I got my wish.

For decades what I knew about foxes, woodchucks, skunks, otters, minks, muskrats, raccoons, squirrels, possums, mockingbirds, and jays came from Thornton Burgess. It certainly didn't come from observation—not in El Paso—or from ecology courses, which I never took. It didn't come from hunting or fishing or camping, for sure.

Thornton Burgess portrayed the fox, the woodchuck, the skunk, and their friends as people in order to attract young readers like me and to get us to appreciate the workings of nature. He was successful. His depiction of the woods as crowded with lively, busy, smart animals stayed with me for a lifetime.

However, Thornton Burgess gave me more than an understanding of the woodland animals' behavior. He gave me a conviction that raccoons, squirrels, jays, and all the other furry, feathery, and hairy animals of Earth were individuals who could feel hunger, pain, sorrow, fear, and joy; individuals who played, cared for their young, and thought about the day's encounters; individuals who remembered who had harmed them and who had helped.

Thornton Burgess made the children who read his books better members of nature's family.

I hope that *Ruminations on a Parrot Named Cosmo* will do for adult readers what Thornton Burgess's books did for children.

Photo by Alvaro Santistevan

Betty Jean Craige retired from the University of Georgia in 2011 as University Professor of Comparative Literature and Director of the Willson Center for Humanities and Arts.

Over four decades Betty Jean wrote numerous books, including the biography of a remarkable human, titled Eugene Odum: Ecosystem Ecologist and Environmentalist, and the shorter *biography of a remarkable bird, titled Conversations with Cosmo: At Home with an African Grey Parrot.* She curated museum exhibitions of the lithographs of Alvar Suñol—at the Georgia Museum of Art and the Albany (Georgia) Museum of Art—and created the documentary Alvar: His Vision and His Art (2006).

For two years Betty Jean wrote a column in the Athens Banner-Herald titled "Cosmo Talks," about her parrot Cosmo. Then she turned her attention to fiction and published four Witherston Murder Mysteries: *Downstream, Fairfield's Auction, Dam Witherston,* and *Saxxons in Witherston*—and a thriller about genome therapy titled *Aldo.*

Betty Jean enjoys traveling, cooking, entertaining, reading, seeing movies, and chatting with her beloved Cosmo.

See: http://www.bettyjeancraige.org/